Praise for *Conversations for Creating Star Performers*

"Shawn Kent Hayashi asks a profound question—'are you inspiring?' Then through practical, real life examples, she demonstrates how leaders can develop from being *motivational* to *inspirational* through the power of conversations. Shawn's energy, enthusiasm, and passion for developing star talent come through in a practical and impactful guide for leaders at all levels."
—Meghan Seybold, executive leadership development
American Express

"Every organization has star performers; however, not every organization is successful in developing them. Shawn's book provides a toolkit and guide for managers to maximize their talent. She artfully leads you through how to engage in effective conversations with your employees to provide them with valuable feedback and development plans to leverage their strengths and obtain peak performance. This is a must read for anyone who wants to cultivate their star performers!"
—Kelly A. Morello, SPHR, senior director, human resources
Clinical Financial Services, LLC

"*Conversations for Creating Star Performers* is a must read for anyone who wants to be an outstanding, inspiring manager, coach, and leader."
—Robyn Helmer-Tallon, vice president HR, Peabody Energy

"If you want more top performers on your team, follow Shawn's sage advice. She shows you how to coach your people to achieve even more than they thought was possible."
—Jill Konrath, author, *SNAP Selling* and *Selling to Big Companies*

"To be a world-class developer of talent you could spend years watching the best, or you could save yourself lots of time and read this book."
—D.A. Benton, New York Times bestselling author, *Executive Charisma* and *CEO Material: How to Be a Leader in Any Organization*

"Shawn has done it again, producing a wonderful book covering such topics as identifying passions, development areas, and blind-spots, and the skills to help you develop star performers on the job and off."
—Jeff Davidson, "The Work-Life Balance Expert®" and the "60-Second Self-Starter"

"A great book for taking stock and asking, am I developing star performers and high performing teams? Shawn shows you how, one conversation at a time. This is a must-read for all managers who are ready to develop their high potential employees and transform them into star performers. With a clear, practical and engaging style, Shawn guides you to master the art of conversations that not only helps you develop your employee talent and you'll also develop your own."
—Evelyn Montalvo, executive coach

Conversations
for Creating
STAR
Performers

Other books by Shawn Kent Hayashi

Conversations for Change®: 12 Ways to Say It Right When It Matters Most

Mastering Your Influence™

The Influence Journey™

The Organized Communicator

Power Presentations: How to Connect With Your Audience & Sell Your Ideas

Conversations
for Creating
STAR
Performers

*Go Beyond the
Performance Review
to Inspire Excellence
Every Day*

SHAWN KENT HAYASHI

New York Chicago San Francisco Lisbon London Madrid Mexico City
Milan New Delhi San Juan Seoul Singapore Sydney Toronto

1 2 3 4 5 6 7 8 9 10   DOC/DOC   1 6 5 4 3 2 1

ISBN   978-0-07-177994-4
MHID   0-07-177994-9

e-ISBN 978-0-07-177995-1
e-MHID   0-07-177995-7

Talent@Work is a registered trademark of Shawn Kent Hayashi.
Conversations for Change is a registered trademark of Shawn Kent Hayashi.
Mastering Your Influence is a trademark of Shawn Kent Hayashi.

McGraw-Hill books are available at special quantity discounts to use as premiums and sales promotions or for use in corporate training programs. To contact a representative, please e-mail us at bulksales@mcgraw-hill.com.

This book is printed on acid-free paper.

Contents

Acknowledgments

There are so many people to thank—a book like this does not come together as a solo effort!

First, a big thank you to all my coaching clients, to the participants in my workshops and seminars, and to the readers of my book *Conversations for Change: 12 Ways to Say It Right When It Matters Most* and the readers of my *Communication Tips* e-mails. I am grateful for your stories, questions, and ideas. Because my work is often confidential, I am not listing your names here. Please know I am grateful and honored for the opportunity to serve you.

Thank you to Michelle Staas and Michelle Martinez for keeping me on track in my office. Thank you to William Hagan and Amit Mallik—you are wonderful marketing interns, and I hope we'll continue to work together during your summers in college.

Thank you to Bob Diforio and the great team at McGraw-Hill: you are a joy to work with, and I look forward to many more projects together.

To my cherished friends and family, I am grateful for our ongoing conversations. Thank you.

John, Alex, Kyle and William, thank you for creating wonderful family time. Jim Hayashi, I am deeply grateful for all your support and encouragement.

Introduction

Are you a coach, manager, or leader who wants to develop star performers? You are now holding the right book in your hands to guide you in doing so. Here you will clearly learn how to engage people in their work. Several specific types of conversations, over time, create the foundation for developing star performers. I'll show you how to confidently create each type of conversation so that you develop a highly engaged team of star performers. You will learn my best secrets for being an outstanding coach and developer of high-potential people.

According to one of my favorite people, Steve Hart, assistant vice president, human capital management, at the Philadelphia Federal Reserve Bank, "Energizing the soul at work and inspiring engagement is really about conversations. The quality of the conversations that leaders engage in with their employees is what makes the difference and leads to a highly productive team." Steve and I talk about this regularly because it is a passion for us, as we are committed to supporting people to develop their talent at work.

This book is about the conversations you'll need to have to deeply engage people—your team members and your peers—and develop star performers at all levels in your organization.

Meet the Managers

Let me introduce you to several people who will bring these conversations alive with me throughout the book.

Nancy, Director of Marketing

Six months ago, a global company known as the world leader in its industry hired Nancy as a director of marketing. Like her boss and this global giant organization, Nancy also aspired to be the best. Her new boss hired her because she saw a world-class drive in Nancy. She was hired to raise the bar in her department and further develop what the next level of excellence would look like.

However, after a while, a challenge arose, which was that Nancy's high standards for herself and her team members were causing trouble in her building peer relationships. Her peers saw her as a change agent bringing in loads of unwanted, new ideas to make what they referred to as "busywork" by replacing processes that had been working just fine. These peers were ready for Nancy to go back to where she had come from, which caused Nancy to reach out to me and ask for coaching.

Nancy wanted to turn things around quickly with her peers and her staff, but she did not know how to do this. Already a high-performing star in marketing abilities, Nancy was now asking to develop her own interpersonal relationship building abilities. Nancy's question was: "How do I go about building strong relationships with peers and team members so that they want to collaborate with me?"

Victor, Vice President of Finance

After successfully holding three key positions in IT, market research, and operations in a midsized company, Victor was promoted to vice president of finance. He was thrilled by the promotion and excited about making a difference for the company. Victor was known for his analytical abilities—he could grasp the big picture and the details, easily seeing what would be needed in the future. One year into the new position, more than 60 percent of Victor's staff had resigned from the company, complaining in their exit interviews that his leadership style was the reason they had decided to leave. Victor was shocked by this feedback and even more surprised when the vice president of human resources told Victor that he needed to dramatically change his leadership style if he was going to be able to keep employees and his current job.

Victor had succeeded in every position he had ever been in; this was the first time he was stumped and not sure of what to do to resolve the issue. This was also the first time he had had a large team of people he was responsible for leading. Victor made an appointment with the CEO of his organization. "My staff members are leaving, saying my leadership style is the problem," he said. "I realize if I do not fix this, I will not be successful here. I want to resolve this, but I need help because I do not know how to turn this situation around. I've never been in this type of situation before." That was when the CEO called me, saying, "Will you develop our VP of finance? He is a star performer in the analytical and technical aspects of finance. We need him to also be able to lead and engage his staff so they want to do the work in his department." When I first met with Victor, his question was: "Will you show me how to fully engage staff members so they are motivated by the work we do here?"

Angela, Senior Director of Operations

Angela had the respect of both her management and the large group of people who reported to her. She was confident she was being developed to take on the vice president role when it came open soon—the person who was in the role had signaled she was close to retiring. Angela was told several times by senior managers that she was a high-potential performer who was going places. With 5 years of experience as a senior director in her department—2 years more than any other person—and 10 years of experience in the department delivering services, she was by far the most qualified person for the VP role. So why didn't she receive the promotion into the role when it became available?

There was no one ready to take her position!

That's right. Angela's organization hired from outside for the VP opening because there was not someone already developed to take Angela's hands-on, task-oriented role, even though it was clear that Angela was the most qualified and ready for the more strategic leadership opportunity. The CEO explained to Angela that she needed to have people ready to take her role and that the new VP hired from the outside would be moved into a new position once Angela had her own role covered; in other words, she could be promoted only after someone was successfully performing her current accountabilities.

Over the past two years, Angela had not focused on developing someone for her role. Instead, she had focused her energy on being ready for the vice president role. Now Angela was asking, "Shawn, will you help me identify what skills someone needs to be successful in my role and then identify the right people so we can develop them? I need star performers who can take over my role, as well as some of the other manager and director positions, so I am ready in 12 months to move into the vice president role. The people we develop now will be reporting to me once I am promoted. I want stars who have long-term growth capacity because I am never going to be in this place without succession bench strength again!" Angela's summarizing question was: "How can I identify and develop three candidates to provide bench strength for the succession plan in my organization?"

Alex, Director of Sales Operations

As a director of sales operations for a large global company, Alex described each of his employees. He referred to them as "team members" as we discussed his organization during our first coaching meetings.

Bob was one of the 10 employees on Alex's team. Neither Alex nor his boss thought that Bob was a good fit for the position he was currently in. The key accountabilities in the role called for lots of customer interaction. The person in that role needed to be someone who was socially outgoing and directive, someone who reached out to customers to interview them about their thinking and engage them in discussions about their services. Bob was more internally motivated—interested in data, facts, logic, and interpreting research. He liked to review reports in his office and preferred doing this over interacting with customers. Bob did not appear to be confident in interacting with customers in groups, as was required in this role.

A few weeks later, when Alex and I met to continue our coaching work together, Alex shared that he had three primary goals in our work together. One of the three goals was to help Bob become more confident and want to engage with customers. A red flag went up for me as I heard Alex talking about this goal for Bob's performance. I asked, "Is this Bob's goal or your goal, Alex?"

"Oh, it is my goal! I want to lead Bob to behave in a new way so that he can succeed in the role he is currently in. I want to show my boss that I can inspire my employees to make big changes and that they can change to fit the demands of a position." As I listened to this reply, the red flag in my mind was waving boldly. Would you like to know why?

This book explains my conversations over time with Nancy, Victor, Angela, Alex, and others to solve their talent management challenges and to develop star performers.

The Next Level

Whom do you serve by being a coach, manager, and developer of star performers? Whom do you add value to by sharing your story, know-how, and guidance? Are you ready to take it to the next level?

As you are learning, you need feedback, social support, the ability to ask questions, and guidance to know you are on the right track. That is what coaching and development is—helping people to succeed to levels they never imagined possible. Coaching provides committed support that demonstrates how to succeed. Clarity, confidence, commitment, and competence are required. I'll show you how! I will answer your questions and provide you support as you apply these ideas on my Talent@ Work blog. (Go to www.ShawnKentHayashi.com to experience the added benefits you will receive as you read this book.)

Make this framework your focus because, if you master it, your ability to develop star performers will change your life and transform how you serve the world. I want to serve you! I care if you are able to master this ability because it will make a big difference in our world today if coaches, managers, and leaders are committed to developing star performers. You can make a meaningful difference by sharing your expertise.

I will show you how. Now is the time.

Developing star performers begins with conversations for building awareness (Chapter 2) to trigger the insights and desire to grow in a new way aligned with what is expected in the role. I'll show you how to set up this type of experience in Chapter 2. I will also provide you with a bonus check-in: Where are you now? Which of the Seven Career Archetypes describes where you are?

This leads to a need to establish the connection between your desired goals and your own passions. I refer to this as "conversations for identifying motivators." You'll learn about that in Chapter 3.

Have you ever wondered about how to create an effective and motivating development plan that takes your people to the next level of performance? Conversations for creating individual development plans will enable you to know which areas you want to intentionally develop in yourself and which ones you want to delegate to your team members. I'll provide a framework for you to do this in Chapters 4 and 5.

In Chapter 6, I will focus on conversations for developing new skills. This is specific step-by-step guidance enabling you to show or tell the people you are coaching the instructions for them to learn the skills that will enable them to accomplish their desired goals.

Sometimes things do not go the way you expected or desired. Conversations for getting back on track will enable you to do a check–in and turn the situation around. Chapter 7 will give you techniques to deal with tricky spots.

How will you know when the results you are seeking have been accomplished? Conversations for accountability will keep people focused and moving forward. Chapter 8 will give you the language to hold people accountable without turning them off.

Chapter 9 will frame the best ways to think about preparing and delivering a performance review discussion. Your organization may already have a performance management process; if so, it would be wise to integrate Chapter 9's ideas with that existing performance review process.

We all love to feel accomplishment! Conversations for recognition are a vital part of keeping momentum going. Ready to learn how? Chapter 10 provides guidance.

Creating clarity about development for future roles is part of succession planning. When we are aware of the key positions and who is being developed for those roles, we can then have conversations for succession planning such as the ones I will show you in Chapter 11.

Inspiring excellence and some frequently asked questions show up in Chapter 12.

In the Appendix, I'll discuss abilities in 24 areas that we identify in the assessments, which we use as part of the individual coaching work that we do with clients. I'll give you direction on how to set up a conversation and action steps for developing these skill areas:

* Conceptual thinking
* Conflict management
* Continuous learning
* Creativity
* Customer focus
* Decision making
* Diplomacy and tact
* Emotional intelligence

- Empathy
- Employee development and coaching
- Flexibility
- Futuristic thinking
- Goal achievement
- Interpersonal skills
- Leadership
- Negotiation
- Persuasion
- Planning and organization
- Presenting
- Problem solving
- Resiliency
- Self-management
- Teamwork
- Written communication

I have a belief that serves me in my life, which is, "I can figure this out and master it if I am learning from a master teacher—someone who is an expert in what I want to learn." Are you willing to believe this too? If so, we are ready now!

Engaging Star Performers

Imagine yourself having fun—what comes to mind?

Now, consider what causes you to want to perform well at work. Does work trigger the same emotions that playing does for you?

I've asked these questions of hundreds of people. One conversation jumps out at me as I reflect on all the ways people have answered these questions. A bit of background before I share the conversation I had with John as I was volunteering at an Odyssey of the Mind (OM) state competition. I am a passionate volunteer for Odyssey of the Mind. OM is a national creativity building competition for teams that are focused on solving long-term and spontaneous problems. On this particular day, I was matched with a partner whom I had never met before—this was John. He was 20-something and a recent college graduate. In our volunteer role, we were responsible for checking in teams for events and giving them the details about what they would need next. John had a *very* casual style of communicating, and he often appeared uninterested in whatever he was doing. However, after observing him for a while, I realized he really was on top of every detail and knew where each team was in the line-up and what information the team needed next. Despite the opposite appearance, he did feel a sense of accomplishment in what he was doing. John had the process and pace down pat even though he was not projecting himself confidently. His communication and body language with people did not match the results he was producing. He was a star at the tactical work we were doing, but no one would have thought that during an individual conversation with him.

Sometimes John and I were very busy. Other times there was nothing to do. That is when I asked the question, "John, in your work, what causes you to want to perform well?" I could tell from the flash of his smile that he knew his answer immediately: "When my boss is watching, or when the girl I have a crush on is watching. The girl I want to date works in the same place I do." I asked, "If they were here today, what would have been different?" He replied, "Oh, . . . um, I would have shown that I knew what I was doing, and I would have been more friendly to everyone who came up to our table for information." Then I asked, "John, when you are working, do you feel the same feelings that you do when you are playing?" He immediately said, "No! Work is work. I am glad when it is time to go so I can then relax and have fun."

In these conversations in which I've asked people what causes them to want to perform well, I've received two types of responses. Some people, like John, have said they wanted to please or perform for others. John paid attention to his impact only on those he wanted to impress, to people outside himself.

Other people have said they wanted to perform well because they had their own internal standard to live up to. When I asked Olivia the question, "What causes you to want to perform well?" she pulled out a personal statement about what she is committed to in everything she does. Her statement included these points: "Deliver outstanding service in everything I do, remember that I have choices and I can make my own decisions, and be aware of my own feelings and allow them to inform my actions rather than create reactions." Her statement has been a reminder to her of the person she aspires to be every day. She has been internally motivated by this commitment she made to herself. Keeping the commitment has been like a game she plays with herself. For Olivia, it has been fun. She knows she is capable of being a star for her own enjoyment of the feeling that comes from having lived up to her own standards. Olivia has had a conversation with herself about the person she wants to be and how she wants to perform. She has used this personal commitment to meet her own standard for her own performance, while John has been using someone else's views of him to determine his star-ability.

Olivia is playing, and John is working.

John was not focused on or aware of challenging or impressing himself, while Olivia wanted to challenge and impress herself every day. In the long term, Olivia's consistent commitment will cause her to surpass John's level of productivity. As a manager, coach, or leader, what can you do to help your team members internalize the desire to perform well? Ask them! Ask, "What causes you to want to perform well?" After you have heard everything they have to say, ask, "When was the last time you had fun at work? What were you doing?"

Can you get a picture in your mind of your favorite coach?

If you are a manager or a leader who is responsible for developing people, imagine yourself as a coach. Why? Coaches are focused on the following:

- Building effective teams
- Engaging people in their own growth and learning
- Building new skills
- Developing high-potential performers
- Helping performers who want to achieve higher levels of success

Coaches ask questions like the ones I've been asking so that reflective learning occurs. They also explain and demonstrate how to accomplish desired goals. Being a great coach and manager requires knowing how to focus your team members on the right things to produce the desired results.

An Emotional Wake

When I was 20-something, I had a boss who asked me and the other members of the team to write our own individual statement for what each of us wanted to accomplish in the upcoming year. He asked us to think about what we wanted to be outstanding at doing and to write a personal statement of commitment. Then he asked us to use the Be, Do, Then Have formula. Who would we need to *be*, what would we need to *do*, so that we could *have* the desired results? A week later, the boss videotaped each team member sharing his or her own Be, Do, Then Have statement. We watched the videos together, and he gave us our own copy. This activity enabled each person to internalize his or her own motivation to be the kind of performer who would produce the desired results no matter who was watching. It made our work seem like playing a game that was fun. Our emotions were engaged in achieving our goals at work.

Richard Boyatzis, PhD, a distinguished professor from the Department of Organizational Behavior at Case Western Reserve University, walked on stage to deliver the keynote address to an audience of executive coaches (including me) with Aretha Franklin's voice blasting in the background:

> What you want, I got it. What you need, you know I got it . . . All I'm asking is for a little . . . R-E-S-P-E-C-T . . . Find out what it means to me . . . R-E-S-P-E-C-T. Take care, ohhhh, Sock it to me . . . A little respect, oh yeah.

As he danced wildly, clapping his hands above his head on stage, he shouted that great leaders move us through our emotions. Learning retention is higher when we engage the brain with music and humor. As a manager and leader, you may often wonder how to inspire people to work on what would be beneficial to them. Great leaders understand that emotions are the connectors that engage people. Employees are not persuaded by your logic and data. Instead, they take action based on their emotions, and then they use the research to justify their actions. Emotion is what causes change.

For over 30 years, Dr. Boyatzis has been researching what causes sustained desired change. He says that arousing, invoking, stimulating, and provoking the desires to develop and change require openness, adaptability, and tolerance for ambiguity. To get to the place in ourselves where we are open like this, we are triggering what he calls the "parasympathetic nervous system, or the Positive Emotional Attractor."

Whom do you most enjoy coaching and developing? Who is drawn to your inspiring words of wisdom? When you reflect on your own expertise and content, what is it specifically that you help others to achieve in an excellent way? Being inspiring and sharing new skills are foundational to being a world-class coach because that is what triggers the Positive Emotional Attractor.

You know how to solve problems. The people you are developing have a problem or challenge that they want assistance in moving through. Your perspective, your past experience, your know-how are valuable to giving clarity and direction in solving challenges, right? People do not believe the message or the learning if they do not believe the messenger. Have you made the connection yourself about the ways in which you can confidently add value by sharing your research or experience? I'll show you how to do this and how to be an outstanding coach!

Change is at the heart of all development because in order to develop new abilities, we take new actions. In my coaching and seminar Talent@Work, I ask participants to identify someone who changed them by bringing out the best in them. Who created a climate that changed your desire so that you wanted to be the best version of you that is possible? Do you notice that when this happened, you were focused not on merely getting by, but rather on being a shining star? Think about managers or leaders who have brought out the best in you. Then think about people who did the opposite, people you went out of your way to avoid:

- Who brought out the best in me?
- Why were they able to do so? What did they do?
- How did I feel when I was with them? Or after I left them?
- Which leaders have brought out the worst in me?
- Why were they able to do so? What did they do?
- How did I feel when I was with them?

On the list of descriptions of people who have brought out the best in you, you probably said something like the following statements:

1. She was growing and sharing what she was learning with the team.
2. He was collaborative and listened to my ideas.
3. I felt valued by him.
4. She was passionate about the work.
5. She was confident.
6. He was future oriented, and he focused on solutions and how to implement them.
7. He asked great questions that encouraged me to think in new ways.
8. She was thoughtful and showed interest in what I was doing.
9. Trust built up in our relationship over time.
10. I felt hope and a sense of possibility.

On the other list, the people who have brought out the worst in you, we would likely see some of these comments:

1. He was very critical and judgmental—I always felt like I was doing something wrong.
2. She was distant and aloof, and she seemed cold or unwilling to engage.
3. He was too rules focused.

4. She seemed exasperated, frustrated, and annoyed much of the time.
5. He was self-absorbed.
6. I felt controlled by needing to please her.
7. He seemed angry and constrained, often complaining.
8. She focused only on problems and risks and what was being done wrong.
9. I did not feel like he cared about what I was doing.
10. She compared me to others and explained how great they were, but she did not share with me how or why this was relevant to me.

Notice how these reflect an emotional wake? When people inspire and lead us, they usually have a positive emotional wake. Emotions are contagious, and we catch the other person's emotional marinade as it spills over onto us. On the other hand, when someone shuts us down and squashes our growth, we experience a negative emotional wake. Leaders who know how to be effective coaches inspire us to new, higher levels of performance (see the box "Are You Inspiring?").

Are You Inspiring?

The word *inspire* literally means to breathe life into. To inspire others, you have to know what motivates them, and you have to be inspired yourself about the topic you are discussing. To be a leader and developer of others, you have to be inspiring. Motivation creates momentum. Flat, monotone, boring, same old same old is not inspired leading. Do you lift people up emotionally by the conversations you have with them? Do you inspire them to see new possibilities for growth? Do your conversations develop star performers who create the next possible vision for your business's growth? That is leadership.

Do you help people connect their long-term goals to the work they are doing today? That is inspiring. That feels like playing. That gives work purpose.

7

(continued)

Neuroscience research shows that when we are using the part of our brain that is about analyzing numbers and data, we have to shut down the part of our brain that engages others emotionally. In other words, don't begin with the spreadsheet data. Instead, start with a conversation about why this project is important for your listeners' long-term goals and for the business. Let that conversation bubble up. After it is crystal clear why this topic is important for personal and business reasons, you can review the spreadsheet to identify the data's connection to the value that is important to the individual or team you are working with. Describe the connection between the two, and do not assume others have connected the dots in the same way you have. Too often we've seen managers begin their conversations with the spreadsheet data and the steps in the procedure manuals—that approach is not engaging.

Emotions are contagious. If you are feeling angry much of the time, your staff will know that. If you are feeling hopeful much of the time, your staff will know that too. Emotions are not hidden by a smile. The chemical marinade we are swimming in is making up our current emotional state, and it impacts our thoughts and word choices, whether we realize it or not. Human beings are hardwired to pick up others' emotions. What you are feeling inside is impacting the outside whether you want it to or not. Emotional intelligence is a foundation skill area for anyone who aspires to be a developer of star performers.

Employees do not trust managers who toe the company line but do not believe it. One of my coaching clients told me she has identified the phrase her boss uses when he does not believe what he is repeating from company information or when he is passing down something he has been told to say. When he thinks it is ridiculous, he conveys that without saying so directly. Then she has to decide how to handle this mixed message, and she feels jammed up and stuck.

We all have annoying things that happen every day—the customer wants it scanned, not faxed, and you don't have access to a scanner; then you spill cranberry juice on your fresh white blouse as you are walking into an important meeting. These little stresses trigger cortisol, a hormone that will be released by the adrenal gland into the emotional chemical marinade we are swimming in. Cortisol has three nasty side effects:

1. Shuts down your immune system
2. Stops neurogenesis, meaning that the brain cannot heal itself by creating new nerve tissue
3. Makes you retain and gain weight

So how do you inspire someone to be open to explore positive change without triggering the levels of fear or anger that cause unhealthy, high levels of cortisol?

Many people may realize when they are feeling stressed, but they likely do not know how to make the shift within themselves into renewal, where they are marinating in positive emotions. Do you? Do you know how to inspire others to do this?

Expressing gratitude triggers a feeling of more gratitude and moves us away from the stress response. Look for times to say and feel, "Thank you!"

The Promise of Coaching

Are you curious about the changing landscape of business and how coaching has become an integral part of helping leaders to develop new competencies needed to adapt and meet today and tomorrow's business challenges? John Kotter in *The Leadership Factor* said that 53 percent of executives do not have the skills to do their job adequately. Most need to be coached to master how to build relationships that engage, develop, and inspire their employees.

It is not the analysis, auditing, or metrics that cause a company to be great. Consider this: the company Enron was audited monthly, yet it failed painfully. We want to add value and to make a difference. We want to feel like we are doing what we were born to do. Effective leaders create a relationship through conversations that engage their followers. The quality of the relationship we have with our employees and teams is based on the intentional, developmental conversations we create with them over time. If you are someone who loves to look at and track measurement results, numbers, and analyses, it is vital that you also learn how to connect with people on an emotional level, not just on a numbers level, if you aspire to develop a high-performing team or organization.

Asking, "What can I do to be helpful?" is a nice gesture, but to make a difference, that sentiment needs to be part of an ongoing conversation. Just offering to help a person does not make a difference or produce positive change. Studies of drug and alcohol abusers show they can get detoxed in a matter of weeks, but if the relationships and the conversations going on around them do not change dramatically, they will be back at the same behaviors that caused them to land in rehab within six months. For their behaviors to change, there has to be a system of support around them. A one-time or one-week effort will not help them. The same is true in turning mediocrity into greatness or poor team performance into high team performance.

What does make a difference?

1. Creating and maintaining ongoing conversations that communicate the purpose of the organization
2. Having conversations that describe the key accountabilities and expectations of each role
3. Asking questions that cause people to explore and find the connections between their own motivation and the organization's purpose
4. Inspiring hope and vision for a new possibility
5. Having conversations that demonstrate compassion, understanding, and empathy
6. Paying attention to health and wellness in the body, mind, and spirit
7. Maintaining ongoing conversations for learning—that is, conversations that help employees increase their

knowledge of their present roles and their possible future roles

8. Having conversations that trigger feelings connected to why people are doing what they are doing

Creating Positive Change

As a manager, you want everyone on your team to be experiencing a positive change and momentum. Moments of starts and stops—a few steps forward, then a sense that nothing is happening, and then moving forward again—are typical during the beginnings of positive change. When we develop, we are creating change. We need to be patient with ourselves during this scrambled time, which will have many steps forward accompanied by a step backward here and there.

Times of personal change are rather similar to cooking, say, scrambled eggs. We start with the yolks and the whites in the shells—not where we want them, so time for a change. We crack the eggs open, and runny liquid spills out into the pan. With a fork we mix the eggs together to create a new consistency and color in the liquid mixture—still not where we want it. We have to be patient and confident, knowing that the desired results are on the way. As the eggs begin to cook, lumps form, but the runny mess is still all over the pan and not where we want it. After waiting and stirring for a few minutes, the eggs take the desired shape and consistency as yummy scrambled eggs. When we go through a change in our abilities, the same process occurs. Discovering who you want to be—what kind of coach, leader, or manager you want to be—occurs in fits and starts as we go through, as I describe them to my coaching clients, the "scrambled egg phases." This is development.

You can help this process along by creating your own learning agenda and finding a caring person to nurture you in your journey. Finding a role model to inspire a vision for your ideal self is useful. A role model can help you to see who you are or who you can be. A role model can help you consider new possibilities for your development and growth. Find someone who is able to believe in you and help you grow, someone who knows how to develop and coach you based on your strengths and natural talents.

People don't want to be fixed! When we slip into trying to fix other people, it does not work because people don't want to feel as if they are broken and must be fixed. People do want to grow and learn. There is a subtle shift in the mindset behind these two stances.

How can you tell when you are in a positive state of development and growth versus a negative state of development and growth—that is, a fix-it state?

Here's a list of traits that go along with a Positive Focus on Development and Growth:

1. I have a vision of my ideal self.
2. I know what triggers my hopes and joys.
3. I am playing to my strengths and the ways I contribute best.
4. My development plan is based on my own goals to grow into the level of performance I desire for myself.
5. I am focused on creative solutions.

Here's a list of traits that go along with a Negative Focus on Broken and Must Be Fixed:

1. I am focused on what triggers my fears and anger.
2. My focus is pessimistic and criticism based.
3. I am working with a Performance Improvement Plan because I am not meeting others' expectations.
4. I am focused on problems.

To be receptive to new ideas and to develop and grow, we have to be in the first state—open and positive focused.

This is why I provide 360-degree assessment data AFTER the people I am coaching have created their own vision of the people they want to be. Then I encourage them to review the feedback from others after they know what they want for themselves. After I see what they have written in their own learning journal, I ask them questions like these:

1. What do you want your life to be like?
2. What is your ideal view of yourself?
3. What is on your That's for Me! list?
4. What are the values that are most important to you?

At that point, they have an ability to internalize the feedback and look for ways it can help them reach their own goals.

There is also great power in *positive imagining*. Visualize yourself living your dreams. See it like a movie playing on the projector in your mind. We cannot inspire passion in others if we have not engaged it in ourselves. You have to be a life-long learner yourself to be an inspiring coach and developer of other people.

Summary

Fixing people does not work. Nor do auditing and measurement because they turn off the brain's relationship building switches. So how do you create sustainability and keep yourself moving forward? The answer is to remember the hope, joy, and love that will come from meeting the desired goal—this is what triggers passion and makes you feel most alive. When you do this, everyone around you will feel it too! The energy is exciting and contagious. We all want to grow.

Are you developing other people for their current roles or for future roles? Either way, you will find a direction and a path in this book. So let me now tie the themes together and point out the types of conversations we need to know how to create in order to help ourselves and others to develop. These are the types of conversations that trigger professional and personal development now and for the future.

Are you ready?

Begin Your Learning Journal

Since you are here to become a better leader and developer of star performers, I'd like to ask you a few questions. Learning requires taking time for self-reflection.

Imagine my saying to you, "I'll be a sounding board for you. I'm inviting you into a conversation that creates the space for your own self-reflection. Please create a learning journal to use during our conversations with each other."

Take the time now to write your own answers:

1. What is my goal (or goals) in reading this book and learning how to develop star performers?
2. What specific outcomes do I want to create for myself and others?
3. What possibilities are available for reaching my goals?
4. Looking at each option, I should consider it from this perspective: "If I do this, then what will happen? Then what?"
5. Reflecting on what I have written, I need to ask myself, "Where do I really want to begin now?"
6. What does Be, Do, Then Have mean for me now?
7. Am I willing to start where I am now? (When would "now" be the right time to begin being a masterful coach and developer of star performers?)

Update Your Learning Journal

As you read this book, update your learning journal. Consider this to be a conversation with yourself about your own growth as a star professional and coach. When was the last time you had a really good conversation with yourself? A learning journal sets the stage for you to grow by asking questions that enable you to reflect. Additional questions for you to answer over time in your learning journal include these:

- What do I enjoy doing?
- Where do I feel I add the most value?

- What are the successes I am most proud of?
- What worked well?
- What did not work well?
- What have I learned from the mistakes I've made?
- What do I want to accomplish next?
- What matters most to me?
- What matters to my boss, to my department, and to my team?
- What will it take for us to accomplish our goals as a team?
- What do I want to learn next?
- What do I want to do differently so that I can focus on the desired learning?
- What do I need to stop doing so that I can have what I desire?
- Imagine that I have been promoted to the next level: What would that look like? How would I need to think differently? What would I need to let go of?

And if you want to develop your emotional intelligence, ask yourself these questions:

- What am I feeling now?
- What triggered that feeling?
- What are the physical and mental symptoms of the feelings I am marinating in now?

Spend three to five minutes per day answering a question or two from this list. You may want to return to a question several times to let your answers keep bubbling up. I asked myself the question "What do I love to do?" over and over for months until the answer was crystal clear for me. I love to develop star performers!

Review Your Learning Journal
Each month, review your learning journal by reading past entries to observe the development of your thinking and beliefs during that time. At the end of the year, it is useful to reread the

whole journal and summarize which insights have held the most significance for you as you have learned to create meaningful conversations for developing star performers.

When you use this process, you will see a positive and dramatic step up in all aspects of your life. As you develop star performers, you will also continue to step up your own abilities and expand your own life.

If you are a coach or manager who is primarily focused on developing your team members or clients, I recommend that you keep your own learning journal and that the people you are working with do the same. This reflective learning space is invaluable in triggering deeply meaningful conversations during coaching meetings. Having your own journal will enable you to share your own stories of what you are learning. Perhaps most important, your stories will be inspiring to the people you are coaching to see that you are a committed life-long learner yourself.

And, yes, I do this! Every morning I begin the day by writing in my own journal what I want to create and my reflections on where I am and where I am going. This quiet time in conversation with myself sets the tone for the day. This conversation determines my emotional state. During this time, I also remind myself of what I am committed to. This is a powerful habit that keeps me focused on what I want to do to learn and live the life of my dreams. You can do this too, starting now!

Conversations for Building Awareness

Before we get into the heart of this chapter, let's start by looking at some questions about effectiveness:

- What is star performance?
- What does it mean to be effective in your current role?
- Who decides what being effective is in your position at work?
- What makes one person more effective than another? Why?

Being effective could be described as meeting the goals or key accountabilities for a role. When a position has clear accountabilities and goals, measuring effectiveness is then possible. Too many times, we've seen positions at work that do not have clearly defined and measurable key accountabilities. When this happens, effectiveness is subjectively based on how the manager feels about the employee rather than what the position needs to drive growth for the organization.

One of my coaching clients from a pharmaceutical company talked to me in depth about his concerns, some of which were these:

- He was unclear about what was expected of him from his boss or peers.
- He was doing the job of three people.
- He was unclear about what people's roles really were.
- He was not sure about what he was accountable for.
- He did not know what would make him a top performer.

When we talked, it was impossible for the client to say if he was a star because no one had distinguished what that meant for the roles in the department in which he worked. I felt his pain! It does not have to be this way. We can solve this so that any of your people can become star performers.

If you are a manager and leader in an organization, one of your first responsibilities is to ensure that you have written accountabilities and goals for those who report to you. I am not talking about job descriptions that are general overviews of the types of work done by the department—those have their place, but this is not it. I am referring to clearly defined accountabilities that answer three questions:

1. Why does this position exist in our organization now?
2. What will this position be responsible for?
3. What will the people who perform in this role really be held accountable for?

By creating a conversation to discuss what effective performance looks like, sounds like, and rewards in each of the accountabilities, we raise awareness about the expectations for the person in the role. We create the possibility of developing star performers!

People do not know what they do not know. In other words, incompetence does not even realize it is incompetent. Awareness building conversations help to fill in the gaps and show people what would be useful for them to focus on next for their own development in their current role. It also helps them begin to think about where they may want to grow to next.

Awareness of expectations is vital to success. We provide this awareness to employees with a Talent Audit or Job Benchmark. What this means is really understanding exactly what is expected of the role: what communication style is best suited to the work that is being done, what values and motivators are rewarded by the work that is being completed, what natural talents are necessary for success in the role, and what level of emotional intelligence the role requires. When we complete a Talent Audit or Job Benchmark for a specific job or role, we clearly identify what it takes to be successful.

I am an avid believer that the foundation of a strong talent pool is clearly defined and benchmarked jobs. Accurately measuring performance in a specific role is possible only after a clear standard for performance has been established. Ideally, every position in an organization has key accountabilities and a benchmark showing the accountabilities, skills, attitudes, motivators, behavioral style, and experience that each position requires for success. If this is in place, then unbiased management can occur.

Creating Job Benchmarks

The way we create Job Benchmarks is by inviting the key stakeholders and the team of subject matter experts to collaborate on defining the position. (See also the box "Online Benchmarking Assessment.") The expert team includes the position's supervisor, the senior manager, and perhaps one or two of the top performers in the role, if there are any. It could also include customers and peers who rely on the role to complete their work. This team does not include every person who is currently in the role, as that could lower the bar for success. We want to identify the star performance, not the average performance.

This benchmarking process realigns the position with the most up-to-date strategic business initiatives. The team members define why the job exists and how it fits into the organization's ongoing strategy (or determines if it is even necessary now given the changes that may have occurred over the past

Online Benchmarking Assessment

You can go online and experience our Talent Audit Job Benchmarking online assessment.

To use the assessment tool, first create the list of key accountabilities needed for your role.

Then complete the online assessment. It will take you about 40 minutes.

If you are uncertain about an answer, look at the TOP key accountability for the role and ask, "If someone were highly successful in that accountability, which answer would be correct?"

Your e-mail address will be necessary for us to provide you the results of the Job Benchmark.

Notes

First, this offer is good for a ONE-time use.

Second, if you choose to have the key stakeholders to a role also complete the Job Benchmarking assessment for your role, we will provide you with a special link and the best version available (executive, sales, management, general, and so on)—that is, the one that aligns with the type of role you are benchmarking. In this case, there will be a fee for the assessment use and a phone consultation to debrief you and the team on the results.

Here is how you may experience the Job Benchmark assessment now as a gift from me for reading this far:

1. Go to www.TheProfessionalDevelopmentGroup.com/Surveys/.
2. Click the green Take Assessment button that is at the left side of the screen.
3. Enter Response Link: 170727CMP.

Completing a Talent Audit Job Benchmark for a role that reports to you will give you great clarity about what you need and want from star performers in a specific role. If you have questions about using the Talent Audit Job Benchmark for developing your team members, please e-mail info@TheProfessionalDevelopmentGroup.com.

few years). A clear picture of the work begins to emerge as they discuss, weigh, and prioritize the key accountabilities for the role. Then the competencies, motivators, personal skills, and communication style that will best suit the role can be identified. It is vital to select new team members who will fit in and be highly engaged on the team from day 1, this Job Benchmark can also be used to coach existing performers so they understand what is expected of them in the role.

Repeatedly, we've seen organizations go through this process and resolve long-standing conflicts between departments and individuals that arose due to misunderstandings about the expectations of roles. In one company where we benchmarked a role in the marketing organization, there had been a long-standing conflict between the sales and marketing departments. When we did the Job Benchmark and had the VP of sales and the VP of marketing state their expectations, it became clear that they were very different in what they were looking for from the role. The trickle-down effect was a "personality conflict" between the two departments that really was a result of a lack of awareness of the expectations of the two leaders.

When there are such different expectations for a role, it is not likely that people in that role will be successful, and conflicts between team members and departments may arise because of the lack of awareness about the expectations. In the case of the sales and marketing departments we worked with, when we showed the employees the Job Benchmark, which included the expectations for the role in 55 different dimensions, the team members realized the conflict was not really a personality clash, and the issues were resolved. With the new awareness about what someone in the role needed to do to be successful, forward momentum began to occur for both the marketing and sales departments. A high-performing team emerged in the 12 months after this because they were now all looking at the same expectations. This is like an orchestra in which all of the musicians are playing from the same sheet music and understand the expectations of their chair.

Once a Job Benchmark is completed, we can look at each person in the role compared to the different dimensions. By assessing each person, it is possible to see where skill gaps exist so that the individuals may be developed for both their present and future roles. The conversation that results raises the individual performers' awareness about exactly what is expected of them in their role. In addition to intelligence and experience, each person brings a unique combination of values, skills, capabilities, and communication style to the role. Each of these factors has a significant impact on performance, which determines whether the employee is an average or a star performer.

Defining Key Accountabilities

While knowing employees' communication styles is crucial for determining whether they are an appropriate fit for the work to be done in the job, it is a mistake to rely solely on a communication style match. The motivators, capabilities, and acumen that align with the role are vital too.

We've seen some sales organizations attempt to promote people based solely on their communication style. This backfires because it is the motivators and capabilities that may make the biggest difference. Look at the whole job, and look at the whole person, not just one slice, to develop and identify star performers. You can then raise their awareness about why you think they have what it takes to succeed in the whole role.

When positions align with individuals' motivators and communication styles, their job satisfaction increases dramatically. The work being performed taps into deeply held motivators and values. The result is invigorated job performance that leads to professional development. The assessment I use also shows what the job needs, with regard to 25 capabilities, and where the performers currently are in each of the capabilities.

A high-potential employee is someone who fits the Talent Audit or Job Benchmark for the position and measures above the mean on at least 19 of the 25 capabilities. "Mediocre performers show up on time and meet deadlines without having to be prodded. Star performers go well beyond that, to work in the white spaces of their job description. If they recognize a problem, even if no one else knows about it, they attempt to solve it. They volunteer to help others when they see they have the knowledge that's needed," according to Stephen Blakesley in *The Target—The Secret to Superior Performance*. This ability to take initiative is one of the measures revealed in the assessments I show organizations when using Job Benchmarking.

The first step in Job Benchmarking is to define the key accountabilities for star performance. Here are several examples:

Executive Director of an Association
- Maintain and develop growth of membership to 30,000 members.
- Oversee the financial management of the association, and report the results to the board of directors quarterly.
- Recruit, retain, and train a high-performing team.
- Oversee effective planning and management of association events.
- Use timely communication between boards, staffs, community, government, and affiliated association chapters.

Senior Software Developer
- Troubleshoot, fix bugs, and test new code completed inside project timeframe.
- Analyze appropriate solutions, and determine best application for entire product line. Design before coding based on customer requirements.
- Write quality applications that meet preset performance standards.
- Document code process so that a peer can develop an understanding of what an application does by reading the documentation.
- Make future projections. Research and develop functionality needed two years from now.

23

District Sales Manager's Six Top Accountabilities in Priority Order

- Manage sales force in the Northeast region to deliver the targeted sales revenue number.
- Develop business plans and key account plans.
- Demonstrate industry and market knowledge, and implement and/or execute an engagement model for addressing the local market.
- Recruit, develop, and manage a strong team of talented product specialists, including providing coaching and leadership for the team members as well as taking action to move out people who are not performing in the role.
- Communicate with the large sales organization. Demonstrate the specific information employees need to know about the technology and lead sales training.
- Provide coverage for the larger sales organization if needed.

Sales Representative's Three Top Accountabilities in Priority Order (Reports to the District Sales Manager Above)

- Prospect, qualify, demonstrate, and close sales according to company guidelines to ensure that sales goals are met while maintaining the company's integrity and brand image.
- Work closely with other sales representatives in adapting and improving the sales strategy for specific products.
- Communicate with customers to ensure that their needs are met, and up-sell additional products to meet customers' needs.

If a person loves to solve complex problems and doing so is motivating to him or her, a project that requires solving complex problems will reward his or her value. I'll explain this in more detail later in the book, but for now it is useful to understand that a Job Benchmark will show the motivators that are rewarded by the organization's culture and by the work and the natural talents, communication style, and competencies required to be successful in each of these roles. In the four prior examples, each position rewards very different motivators and communication styles.

Here is another example showing each accountability with its rank and weight:

Sales Manager

Category	Key Accountability Statements	Rank	Percent of Job
A	Accurately set the sales forecast and manage the strategic and tactical sales process from beginning to end in order to meet sales goals.	1	50%
B	Effectively lead, develop, and manage sales team in order to accomplish business objectives.	2	20%
C	Effectively manage and use customer activity in order to gain market share and ensure superior customer satisfaction.	5	5%
D	Effectively manage dealer activity to gain market share and understanding of market conditions.	4	20%
E	Share and transfer sales data and market intel to internal personnel to influence enterprise business decisions.	3	5%

Writing Your Own Goals

As an individual performer who wants to be highly effective, are you able to put your hands on your written goals for your current role? If so, are you aware of what you need or want to develop to be a star? If not, there is a conversation that has been overlooked.

Your first coaching assignment is to write your accountabilities and goals. Then discuss them with your manager, if you have one. If you do not have a manager, that means you are the leader and perhaps the owner of the organization. In that case, it is vital that you have clearly defined accountabilities for you to lead the cause. I also suggest you share your accountabilities and goals with your own personal board of advisors. Your team needs to know your accountabilities and be updated regularly on your progress.

Having accountabilities and goals is an indicator that someone is committed to creating momentum in life. People who are most effective at work think and talk about their goals every day.

To raise your own awareness about what you want to create, I have a challenge for you:

Challenge

Create a list of 100 things, services, opportunities, and conversations you want to create. On your list include conversations you want to experience with your coworkers, friends, and family; things you would like to own that you do not have yet; skills you want to develop; places you want to visit; and people you want to meet.

When I was first asked to create a list like this, I thought 100 sounded like way too many. I came back to the next coaching meeting a week later with 20 items on my list and happily told my coach I had completed the assignment. My coach said to me, "Shawn, why did you create a glass ceiling for yourself? I offered you a bigger vision, and you kept it smaller. By limiting yourself to only 20, you created your own glass ceiling that will limit what you can create for yourself. Don't come back until you have 100 items on your list." I could not imagine why this list of 100 was so magical, but I wanted to keep working with my coach, so I made the list. I noticed when I reached items in the 80s and 90s on my list, I was thinking in a much bigger way for myself. I was also aware of conversations I wanted to create with coworkers and family members that I had never thought of before. I began to call my list the That's for Me! list. It is like having your own agenda for yourself.

Daydreaming about what we want to create takes time. Over the next week, take this challenge yourself. Once you are in the habit of reviewing your own list regularly, you will begin to see the magic that flows from the self-awareness. Your goals and the corresponding accountabilities will become clearer to you and to others because you will talk about what is on your list. You will begin to use the list to direct your free time. What would I like to do today? Hmm, let me check what is on my That's for Me! list. Your boss asks you where you want to focus your professional learning budget for the year—you already know the answer because you wrote it on your That's for Me! list. Some of my coaching clients call their list "My Agenda." Where would I like to go on vacation? Oh, let me get out my That's for Me! list to see what is there.

This is thinking about whom you want to become and where you want to grow. You become self-aware. Which projects and assignments you want to engage in become clearer as you do the steps to know yourself, your interests, and what inspires you. If you do not know how to do this for yourself, you will not be able to inspire the people you are developing to become clear in their own goals. Our ability to set goals for every part of our lives is vital to creating star performance in all areas. If we do not do this ourselves, we will not be able to role model it for others. Excitement, energy, and passion can fill our work in a way that draws new team members to want to be on our teams only when we make the connection and use this skill consciously as leaders ourselves.

Helping Your Employees Stay Aware

As a manager, ask your employees to create their own That's for Me! list. Once they know what they want for the next several years, they will be able to connect the dots on why the work they are doing now will help them to grow and develop in a way that is meaningful to them. High performers are engaged in their key accountabilities and goals at work because they understand how it will help them experience something that is meaningful to them.

In January, I asked my employees how they would use their bonus if they earned the full bonus number. I asked them to write exactly what they would do if they reached 100 percent of their bonus potential. One team member wanted a new pearl necklace, another wanted to save the money for her son's college fund, another wanted to go on a large game hunting trip with a group of friends, and the list went on. At our first staff meeting of each month, I asked them to come prepared to share what they had done and were doing to ensure that they met their goal. At the end of the year, they had earned 120 percent of their bonus pool! I am certain this happened because we created the structure for success and maintained an ongoing conversation for accountability as a team. We kept their key accountabilities alive by connecting them to their own personal motivations and by talking about them regularly.

Awareness that It May Be Time to Move On

Toni Moore, the former director of North America HR Operations at Wyeth Pharmaceuticals, shared this insightful point in a conversation we had about helping a star performer to be aware of the current reality when his or her developmental desires do not align with the goals of the organization:

> Career advancement may not be available in the organization through no fault of the employee or the organization. This may happen when an employee is midcareer and wants to grow to the next level but has not recognized that the position he or she wants to grow into is not available or that there are several other candidates who are better aligned to move into the role.
>
> A conversation with a currently high-performing employee in which it is stated that the employee has reached his or her growth potential in both the current position and the company is often difficult. While this conversation is not intended to be negative, it can be an extremely sensitive discussion for a manager to begin. You are essentially suggesting that a high-performing employee may want to consider leaving the company if he or she really wants to be promoted into higher-level assignments. It is a difficult conversation for you as a manager because you could potentially lose a high-performing member of your own team if the employee leaves. There may be another type of problem if the employee stays but is

disgruntled that he or she was not selected for the desired role or assignments.

This type of development conversation requires ongoing discussions and performance monitoring for the manager. You do not want to discourage a high-potential employee. It has been my experience that the end result of this type of conversation is often extremely positive. If the employee decides to remain with the current company, he or she understands why he or she may not experience promotions and advancement as quickly. This employee is also not likely to feel discouraged because he or she made the choice for himself or herself to broaden in the role before moving up. If the employee decides to leave, he or she understands it is for career advancement only.

In either case, the manager needs to provide encouragement and continued challenges for this employee until he or she is able to determine the next direction.

Do you have individuals on your team who want to move beyond the role they are in but you realize the organization is not able to give them what they are requesting? Whom do you need to have a conversation like this with?

Putting It into Action: Joan

What could you say to set up a conversation like this?

Joan, you are doing a great job in your current role. You are a star performer, and I appreciate your contributions. I also want to be clear about the current reality in the organization at this time. You shared with me that you want to be developed for the VP of operations role. I understand why that role is of interest to you based on your current skill set and communication style preferences. There are already several other people who are being developed for that role, and the person who holds it is not intending to leave anytime soon that I know of. Of course, things could change, but you indicated you are looking for a growth path that has you in a VP role in the next 12 to

18 months, and I do not see that possibility here in the timeframe you desire. Would you like to discuss how we could adjust to this reality? Perhaps we can both think on this and evolve our conversation over the next two weeks?

Staying Aware of Your Employees

Brad Golden, the CEO of Eastern Research Services, told me that his primary focus is on making sure the right people are in the right roles. Brad is sure that to grow an organization, we have to be aware of the abilities of our team members and ensure that they are in the right roles to add value to the organization. This is his number 1 accountability. In your organization, do the leaders understand the full array of talents of all of their employees so that they know how and when to best deploy their talent assets?

As a manager and leader, it is very important that you are aware of the strengths, blind spots, and developmental areas of each individual who reports to you as well as those you are considering adding to your team. One of my mentors, Bill Bonnstetter, the chairman of the board of TTI Performance Systems, shared research from over 9,000 Job Benchmarks that showed "the price of admission competencies." Bill advised that these are the top five most important competencies your team members should have:

1. Personal accountability
2. Goals orientation
3. Continuous learning
4. Interpersonal skills
5. Resiliency

There's a reason that personal accountability is at the top of that list. Bill told me if you have candidates for a position who do not have high levels of personal accountability, "send them to your competitors."

Putting It into Action: Angela

Let's see what one of these conversations for building awareness looks like in action.

Do you recall Angela? Over the past two years, Angela had not focused on developing someone for her role. Instead, she had focused her energy on being ready for the vice president role. Now Angela was asking me to help her identify the right people so she could develop them. She needed star performers who could take over her role as well as some of the other manager and director positions so she'd be ready in 12 months to move into the vice president role. The people she and her peers developed would be reporting to her once she got promoted, and she understandably wanted stars with long-term growth capacity because she'd never be where she needs to be without the right support. Angela's question was: "How can I identify and develop three candidates to provide bench strength for the succession plan in my organization?"

What We Did

First, we completed a Job Benchmark for Angela's current position. We did this by pulling together her manager and the key stakeholders. We had them discuss the reason why the job exists and the key accountabilities. Then each of them completed an online assessment to identify the 55 dimensions of the job so that we were clear on what the job rewards, what skills must be mastered or developed, and which communication style would be most successful in the role. When we combined the views of the role, we were clear on what the Job Benchmark was. This took less than three hours to complete!

Next, we looked at each member of Angela's team as well as many other teams in her department. We assessed their motivators, talents, and communication style to see which ones were the closest match to what the job needed. The top five people were the ones Angela began to develop for future manager roles. This process saved Angela time and money by streamlining her efforts to develop people who would be a natural fit for the type of work that was needed. She now had a structure and a framework in which to develop people. She knew how to do what needed to be done next. We were able to create customized development plans for each of the five people, and over the next two years, all of them were ready when they were promoted into manager roles. You can do this too in your own organization.

Phrases for Starting a Conversation for Awareness to Develop Star Performers

- What makes you feel most excited in your current role?
- When you look at the key accountabilities for your role, which ones are you most excited about doing?
- If you are not loving what you are doing 80 percent of the time in your current role, let's talk about that and explore what the options may be to help you find a role that would work better for you.
- What projects or tasks would you like the opportunity to explore if your natural talents are a good fit with that type of work?
- When people are engaged in their work and the team they are part of, you can feel the difference. Do you notice that here?

Seven Career Archetypes: Where Are You Now?

People do not stay in one developmental stage forever. As you mature, you naturally want to make changes in your career. People on the fast track typically take a step forward or sideways every 18 to 24 months. Identifying your current archetype is the awareness step in creating an action plan for where you want to go with your career.

I have done a lot of research on how people use *mentors, networks,* and *role models* to grow in their careers. From interviews conducted with over 100 professionals on the subject of career development, I saw a pattern of dynamic career archetypes:

1. Seekers
2. Prodigies
3. Movers and Shakers
4. Steady Progressors
5. Late Bloomers
6. Stabilized
7. Checked Out or Going Nowhere

Let me describe each so you can consider where the people you are focused on developing likely are.

Seekers

These people are looking for new opportunities. They have lots of questions and need inspiration. New college graduates or people emerging from one of the other archetypes may be Seekers. They probably just landed their first professional position and are looking for a career path. Perhaps they left an unfulfilling job to try another industry or role, or they are coming back into the work world after raising a child. Seekers are looking for the right spot to land. Identifying strengths, goals, and personal needs is the next step for the Seekers. Recent graduates, retirees who still want to work, and people changing jobs or industries usually identify themselves as Seekers.

If you have Seekers working on your team, consider giving them these action steps:

- Set goals and have them commit to taking action on them.
- Suggest that the Seekers search LinkedIn to find people who are doing things that inspire them.
- Have the Seekers conduct at least five informational interviews in the next month to learn more about opportunities with people who inspire them.

- Create a career development plan based on their natural talents, workplace motivators, and preferred communication style.
- Suggest that the Seekers post updates to their LinkedIn page that share their goals and interests so that people in their network know what they are looking for.

Prodigies

These are fast trackers who, if they continue on this path, will graduate to Movers and Shakers. They are often on the high-potential or potential partner list within their companies. They are usually promoted, moved into developmental roles, or given additional responsibilities every 18 months to two years. Prodigies are the people who realize that their career development is their own personal responsibility. They seek out a mentor, have a role model, and build an active career network. They usually make it onto the high-potential list in their organization or start their own business, ensuring that they have an opportunity to use a wide variety of skills.

If you have Prodigies working on your team, consider suggesting these action steps:

- Find Movers and Shakers to role model the next steps for them. Join the association meetings or internal workplace clubs where the Prodigies can meet more of the Movers and Shakers.
- Have the Prodigies invite everyone they know professionally into their LinkedIn network, and have the Prodigies regularly share in their LinkedIn status updates what they are doing in their current work roles.
- Have the Prodigies ask the Movers and Shakers what they did to manage the transition from being Prodigies.
- Have the Prodigies network extensively to publicize their work.
- Tell the Prodigies to say yes when their local newspaper and/or industry magazine asks to write an article about their accomplishments. Better yet, have the Prodigies

proactively reach out to journalists who specialize in their field, and have them inform those journalists of their recent professional activities.
- Have the Prodigies regularly thank the people who are helping them learn and have new experiences.

Movers and Shakers

Mover and Shakers are basically the grown-up version of Prodigies. When they were Prodigies, they identified a role model who shared a picture of the people they could be when they matured professionally. The Movers and Shakers have a very large network that they work successfully to fulfill their role. A mentor helped them gain technical skills and competence to manage, but they ended the mentoring part of this relationship when they realized they had outgrown the mentor. Now the Movers and Shakers rely on a wide network to expand their thinking. Others look to them to make things happen. Handling a large responsibility and being comfortable with high visibility are evidence of Movers and Shakers. Partners, vice presidents, and senior-level executives usually identify themselves as Movers and Shakers.

If you have Movers and Shakers working on your team, consider suggesting these action steps:

- Have them choose a mentee who wants to learn what they have to offer and who will help them build a network of tomorrow's success stories. Each year have the Movers and Shakers select new mentees, and watch their networks expand with people who are grateful for the contribution they made to their careers.
- Have them take on leadership roles in their profession's associations at a local or national level.
- Have them read *The Adult Years* by Frederick Hudson to prepare for the next phase in their own career progression.
- *Bonus gift*: Read the article "Mentoring" located at www .TheProfessionalDevelopmentGroup.com/resources/.

Movers and Shakers are invested in what they need to do to grow. They are wise and willing to share their experiences with others.

Steady Progressors

People who have worked for the same company for years, slowly growing and garnering promotions, are Steady Progessors. These folks have been in the same department for over 10 years, and they are satisfied with a promotion rate of perhaps 5 to 7 years before moving into a new role. The Steady Progressors are the people who slowly, deliberately work hard. They are rewarded for their work with opportunities to develop new skills, but they rarely take big risks. Eventually, after decades of intense work, the Steady Progressors may reach senior management, but that option is becoming increasingly rare due to flatter organization structures in which only high-potential risk takers make it to the top. The Steady Progressors often work through lunch without taking a break to build an internal network. They may have a technical mentor and a network of technically competent pals, but they do not let these associates influence their risk taking.

If you have Steady Progressors working on your team, consider suggesting these action steps:

- Have them consider whether this is the path they want to stay on. What is keeping them here: life choice or fear?
- Have them create conversations with several different Prodigies in your organization during which the Steady Progressors listen to their theories on organizational politics, how influence occurs, and what they are doing to move up on the fast track.
- Have them set new goals to meet more people, maintain balance, and intentionally train others to take their position so that the Steady Progressors can assume additional responsibilities.
- Have them learn about organizational politics. Have them read my previous book *Mastering Your Influence Workbook* and

intentionally focus on building stronger interpersonal communication skills (located at www.TheProfesssional DevelopmentGroup.com/store).

Late Bloomers

Late Bloomers are people with a new energy for their career and work; they are inspired by what they can do and create. They may have spent much of their early career becoming competent in a specific body of knowledge. Now, after many years, they realize that being technically competent is not enough to let them reach their goals. They begin to seek out help to discern the parts of business dynamics that they do not understand, and they start to develop a broader career network. Late Bloomers may also be people who spend many years in a blue-collar position and then decide they want to change careers, resulting in the pursuit of a role model, a mentor, and a career network to move into a professional field. Late Bloomers may have been Steady Progressors for years.

If you have Late Bloomers working on your team, consider suggesting these action steps:

- Have them set three specific goals for the next phase, and have them focus on those goals every day.
- Have them attend their targeted industry's association meetings and annual conventions to build a broader network of people at all levels in their field.
- Have them find Movers and Shakers with whom to benchmark and conduct informational interviews. Have them ask themselves how their area of knowledge could add value to the Movers and Shakers, and have them find opportunities to discuss this possibility.
- Have the Late Bloomers find something inspiring in what the Movers and Shakers are doing, and have the Late Bloomers discuss it with them.
- Have them stay in touch with people in their network.

37

Stabilized

Stabilized people have reached a level of success that is meaningful for them, and they have no desire to move, take on additional responsibilities, or change. Stabilized people have other aspects to their life that they are pursuing now. This style inspired the name "mommy or daddy track" to describe professionals who had decided to put their careers on hold to care for children. Other situations can cause people to become Stabilized in their careers. For example, they may be caring for an elderly parent and want to work reduced hours because being there for the loved one takes precedence over anything else. Stabilized people may have come to this point after plugging away and feeling like they had nothing to show for it. They may have been Prodigies who decided that the level of energy it would take to continue down that path was not right for this phase of their life.

Stabilized people feel happy in their job, and they really do not want to grow into another one. They'd be happy staying where they are for several more years or maybe even retiring from this position. Career sales representatives, researchers, and small business owners often identify with this style. Stabilized people may not realize they have been put in this category by their management. If people have not received a promotion or a lateral move in three to five years, they may have plateaued in their current role and are thus Stabilized for now.

If you have Stabilized employees working on your team, consider suggesting these action steps:

- Have them decide how long they want their career to be stabilized based on the other factors in their life.
- Have them evaluate what they want next.
- My book *The Influence Journal* provides questions and direction that can be a great way to start thinking about the kind of influence Stabilized employees want to create.
- Have them create a game plan for getting back into their career path when it becomes appropriate for them to do so.

- Have them determine whom they can be building relationships with or networking with now, so that when it is time to make a change, they will have the contacts to help them.
- Have them stay in touch with people though LinkedIn.
- Have them read a book or industry magazine each month to stay aware of trends and changes in their profession.

Checked Out or Going Nowhere

It is unlikely that anyone from this archetype is reading this book! These people are disengaged and have no goals, no role models, and few contacts. They take no risks, and they do not use or may not be aware of their strengths. The Going Nowhere people tend to put someone else in the driver's seat to define what they do with their time while at work. They may feel tied to the income that they earn in an unfulfilling position, and they see no way out of the rat race they created with financial obligations. Depression, preparing for retirement, or overly demanding family connections may have contributed to this. These people have not yet realized that they are responsible for and are the predominant creative force in their own life. They are waiting for someone else to make it happen for them.

If you have Checked Out or Going Nowhere people on your team, consider suggesting these action steps:

- Have them decide if this is an acceptable place to be.
- Have them commit to taking action to get out of the rut.
- Have them sign up for one-on-one coaching with a career consultant or life coach who will hold them accountable.
- Encourage them to become Seekers and to be curious.

The people you want to develop into star performers need to be aware of where it is they are in their career and where they aspire to be.

The Seven Career Archetypes model can be useful to start a conversation with people you are responsible for developing.

Share the model with them, and ask them where they see themselves in it. Then share your own reaction: where do you see them and why?

Conversations for Identifying Motivators

Star performers are people who have aligned their work to their values so that they are passionate about what they are doing. The glue that keeps people and organizations happily connected to each other consists of their values, also called workplace motivators. Understanding the values of the person or team you are developing will enable you to build rapport and create meaningful connections. Let's take a look at someone who is just such a person, with one hitch holding her back.

Elizabeth

Elizabeth was a star performer on the high-potential track in the huge accounting firm where she had worked for over 10 years. Every 12 to 18 months she was given increased responsibility or a promotion. She enjoyed serving as the controller and aspired to be the chief financial officer. During this time, Elizabeth also served on the board of a nonprofit organization, and she helped that organization revamp its processes and solved some complex problems the organization had been struggling with for many years. Elizabeth felt great about her career and her potential. When the president of the nonprofit organization invited Elizabeth to be the new CFO, she was excited. The first few months in her new role proved to be more difficult than Elizabeth had imagined. And after a year in the new position, Elizabeth was asked to resign from her role. What happened? How could she go from being a high-performing star in one organization to being asked to resign from another?

Walt Disney's brother Roy Disney said, "When your values are clear, decision making is easier." When we know what we believe, we can make our "yes" an authentic "yes!" When we are clear on our values, we say "maybe" much less.

What we want to do and how well we will perform are determined by our values. We will be most interested in projects, teams, and people that align with our own values. Likewise, we will move away from or be resistant to projects and people that are focused on our lowest value.

Elizabeth first worked in an accounting organization that deeply valued return on investment, problem solving, and following the rules. These values matched Elizabeth's workplace motivators. She moved into a nonprofit organization that was mainly focused on helping people, making sure that people felt good about themselves, and being the recognized leader in charitable work. The values of the new organization were not a fit for Elizabeth's own workplace motivators.

The Six Basic Types of Workplace Values

I use the words *values* and *workplace motivators* interchangeably throughout this book because in this context they mean the same thing. According to research done by Eduard Spranger, which he described in his 1928 classic *Types of Men,* there are six basic values that show up in the workplace. (Spranger's research was the basis of G. W. Allport and P. E. Vernon's 1931 Study of Values, which later became a widely used assessment tool.) These are the six values:

1. *Theoretical:* Wanting the answers, facts, data, and truth, and sharing knowledge for problem solving.
2. *Utilitarian:* Wanting things to be useful and productive, and seeking financial well-being; possibly using money or points to keep score. This value is all about practicality and return on investment.
3. *Traditional:* Wanting instructions or procedures so that life can be lived or work can be done correctly.
4. *Social:* Wanting to make a difference for others; wanting to solve people challenges, such as hate, poverty, homelessness, hunger, and political issues.
5. *Individualistic:* Wanting to be at the table when decisions are made; seeking to be a leader whose voice matters; winning and leading in a world-class way.
6. *Aesthetic:* Wanting things to be harmonious; wanting things to feel good, look good, or sound pleasing; artistic, creative, subjective.

Each of us is motivated by our top two or three values; these are what determine why we do what we do. Both our highest and lowest values have a huge impact on our best career path, culture, and success pattern and the types of work we find meaningful.

When our values match up well with a boss, a team, or an organizational culture, we are often seen as high-potential employees. Passion is evident when we share our own values with others in what we are doing. We show up as authentic. We experience the most job satisfaction when we are clear on our values and are making choices that are aligned with them.

Let's explore each of the six values so we can begin to identify them in the people we are developing. It will prove helpful later on to identify your employees who are driven by each type of motivator.

Theoretical

People who are passionate about reading, doing research, solving problems, and working with facts, data, and logic are having fun because of their high Theoretical motivator. Listening to or reading a series of books on a specific topic and watching documentaries on PBS may feel like play and are also likely common activities for this values type. A passion for education and learning are signs that someone is driven by this value.

High Theoretical motivators inspire careers such as these:

- Mathematician
- New product developer
- Market researcher
- Doctor
- Scientist
- Investigator
- Researcher
- Statistician
- Lawyer
- Any other roles that focus on continuous learning

Does anyone work on your team who is motivated by Theoretical drives?

Utilitarian

People with high Utilitarian values want a return on their investment of time, energy, and money. Self-made people who create new products and services for profit have high Utilitarian values. Games like Monopoly, Risk, or Cash Flow mirror the fun people with high Utilitarian values have when working in a role that rewards them for their motivators. A well-known Utilitarian, Ayn Rand, wrote *Atlas Shrugged* based on her philosophy: "America's abundance was not created by public sacrifices to the public good but by the productive genius of free men who pursued their own personal interests and the making of their own private fortunes." This belief is appealing to people with high Utilitarian values who want to be practical with time, money, and resources.

High Utilitarian motivators inspire careers such as these:

- CEO
- Financial officer or advisor
- Salesperson
- Entrepreneur
- Professional organizer
- Banker
- Engineer
- Manager
- Roles that focus on efficiency

Does anyone work on your team who is motivated by Utilitarian drives?

Traditional

Have you ever observed someone who has a system for living? Living by a set of rules and encouraging or prodding others to accept the same standards is common for people with high Traditional values. These rules could be a strong focus on quality processes, laws, procedures, or religious doctrine. The goal with this motivator is to influence others to follow the same traditions. Political activists and fundamentalist religious groups are motivated by this value.

High Traditional motivators inspire careers such as these:

- Pastor
- Wedding planner
- Funeral director
- Firefighter
- Police officer
- Quality control expert
- Teacher

Does anyone work on your team who is motivated by Traditional drives?

Social

Nonprofit organizations, such as Kiva and the Red Cross, were founded by people with high Social values as their primary motivator. For-profit companies can also be driven by the Social value. When you see an organization that puts the welfare of people above its desire to make a profit, you are seeing the Social value in action. Have you ever been part of a group that was focused on doing something for others, such as working with Habitat for Humanity, for example? Wanting to make a difference for others—wanting to solve social issues such as hate, poverty, homelessness, and justice issues—is a clue that someone has high Social values.

High Social values motivators inspire careers such as these:

- Nurse
- Emergency medical technician
- Counselor
- Minister
- Elementary school educator
- Fund-raiser for nonprofit organizations
- Teacher
- Customer service representative
- Firefighter
- Police officer

Does anyone work on your team who is motivated by Social drives?

Individualistic

Corporate and political leaders have in common the Individualistic value; otherwise, they would not be willing to do what it takes to be in a leadership role. The Individualistic value is a drive that will cause people to stand up for what they believe in and make change. When they see how something could be done better, they are willing to initiate changes to make it happen. When you see someone who enjoys leading groups, teams, or committees, you are seeing signs of the Individualistic value in action. Wanting to win, wanting to be at the table when decisions are made, and seeking to be an expert whose voice matters are indications that you are looking at people with high Individualistic values. People who become well known because of their drive typically have this value in the top three.

High Individualistic motivators inspire careers such as these:

- Politician
- Leader of an association or organization
- C-level executive such as CEO, COO, and CFO
- President
- Committee chairperson
- Board member

Does anyone work on your team who is motivated by Individualistic drives?

Aesthetic

When the Aesthetic value is highest, people will put a strong emphasis on form, function, feelings, and the need to be in environments that are beautiful and harmonious to their senses. When people are motivated by high Aesthetic values, they will want things to feel good, look good, or sound pleasing. Some children develop this value at an early age, and they begin to show signs of artistic, design, or musical ability very young. Others may develop this value later in life as other motivations have been fulfilled.

High Aesthetic motivators inspire careers such as these:

- Photographer
- Landscaper
- Chef
- Hairstylist
- Interior designer
- Musician

- Artist
- Physical trainer
- Fashion designer and model
- Jewelry designer
- Fiction writer
- Architect
- Forest service ranger

Does anyone work on your team who is motivated by Aesthetic drives?

Your Employees' Top Values

Let's take a closer look at these values now to see what it means when specific ones are the top values for the people who work for you. If the Individualistic motivator is in the top three values, it will drive those people to want to be leaders. Unlike the other values, the Individualistic value is expressed through the two other values that are close to it on a ranked list of values. In other words, if Individualistic is in the top three values, it acts as a booster to the two that are next to it in the list. So, for example, imagine that Anthony, a director of research, has values ranked in this order:

1. Individualistic
2. Theoretical
3. Social
4. Traditional
5. Utilitarian
6. Aesthetic

Someone with the Individualistic value above the Theoretical and Social may want to become a star performer as a professor at an Ivy League university or perhaps as an award-winning television documentary producer focused on helping people with cutting-edge information. These roles would feel like enjoyable play to a person with this value hierarchy. Individualistic adds the motivation to lead and to be part of what is considered to be the best or world class.

As another example, Mercedes, a new product designer, has these two values first:

1. Aesthetic
2. Individualistic

Mercedes could be passionate about being an award-winning architect, an interior designer, a yoga instructor, a psychologist, or a world-class art collector. People may be on one career path when, as a result of becoming aware of their own motivators, they come to realize they would be more passionate about another path that would play to their strengths better. As a leader, it is vital to be aware of this and to be able to coach people to understand their own motivators. The third value on Mercedes' list will determine which path would be better for her. If she has Utilitarian as her third value, she will be driven to keep score and make progress or earn more money than if she had Social as her third value, which would motivate her to want to help people through a meaningful cause.

The Organization's Top Values

So why is all this information about values so important to being a star performer? There are two reasons. If your people do not know what their values are, they will not be in control of their agenda. In order for us to be able to have our own agenda with goals and motivation, we need to understand ourselves. Our values determine what we are passionate about doing—what will feel like play to us. When we are passionate about something, we are going to focus more effort on doing it well. Our values determine if we will have the drive to see the project through despite obstacles and resistance.

Putting It into Action: Motivators

Create a conversation with the people or team you are developing by asking these questions:

- How would you rank your motivators using the list of six values?
- What does your values hierarchy reveal about your unique interests?
- Are your values being rewarded by the work you are currently doing?
- Together let's explore how your values have motivated the choices you've made about your work and your relationships with bosses and teams.
- What additional assignments could you raise your hand for that would align with your values?

Can you identify the times in your career when you were not motivated? These are likely instances in which the rewards of the project, organization, or boss did not align with your own top three motivators. As we understand the impact our values have had on our own motivation, we can begin to see the impact values have on other people. You can ask questions of others to understand their values. When you have a sense of what other people's values are, you will be able to initiate coaching conversations focused on topics that would be of interest to them.

The second reason it is important to understand values is so that you can see how the employees' values jibe with those of the organizations they are working within.

Corporate cultures have a values profile that focuses the work of the organization. The Memorial Sloan Kettering Cancer Center would have Social and Theoretical as the organization's top values. Harold Varmus, its CEO, probably has high Individualistic values mixed into these two. Omnimedia, the company run by Martha Stewart, appears to have Aesthetic, Utilitarian, and Theoretical values as its core. If you work in these organizations, you'll need to be able to connect to their values. Martha Stewart herself probably has high Individualistic values that have driven her to be as famous and powerful as she is. Understanding the difference between the values of the individual and the values of the organization helps us to communicate clearly. Having the awareness to see the values of an organization and an individual also helps us to know where and with whom we would fit in best.

The Federal Reserve Bank has a very different corporate culture from Sloan Kettering and Omnimedia. Traditional and Utilitarian values drive much of the Federal Reserve Bank's organization. Yet in some departments it is possible to find the predominant values being Social and Theoretical—can you imagine which departments these may be? Community affairs and human resources departments often have Social motivators as their highest values. The people who work in the departments that are not aligned with the overall values of the organization will have to learn how to flex their style to be heard by the organization's leaders, who will probably have different motivators.

When your core workplace motivators match the organization's values, it is more likely you will experience joy in your work. For example, Marco worked in an architectural firm where the top core values were Aesthetic and Theoretical. Marco's top values are Social and Utilitarian. He did not feel recognized or rewarded for his contributions and suggestions. When he admitted this, he decided to make a career change to an organization that would reward his passion for Social and Utilitarian projects. People with high Traditional and Social values will feel like they are beating their head against a brick wall if they go to work in an organization that is driven by Utilitarian and Theoretical values.

This is a conversation I initiate with my own coaching clients very early in our work together. We identify their values hierarchy and the values hierarchy of the organization in which they work so that we understand how they fit in and where their tricky spots will be.

Your values hierarchy impacts how you make decisions and what you want to develop in yourself and others. Think about the conversations you have had that changed the direction of your own career or life. What have been the developmental turning-point conversations for you?

Although it may sound like a very personal question, "What makes you feel most alive?" is a great question to uncover what people value and what will cause them to be passionate about doing a good job at work. You can observe other people's values by asking them what they are passionate about and where they put their time, resources, and money. Michelle, a human resources director, often invites people in her division to participate in the organization's Habitat for Humanity day. She does this with joy because it mirrors her high Social value. If you wanted to get to know Michelle better, you could start by asking her a few questions about one of these projects. She would be delighted to engage in a conversation about the impact working with Habitat for Humanity has had on several of the teams in her organization.

If we are able to think for ourselves, we will develop a values hierarchy. Young people form their values on the playground, in the classroom, and at birthday parties and by watching their parents. They will lock in a values hierarchy by around 20 years old. After that, our values hierarchy may change if we have significant emotional events. Examples of significant emotional events include being promoted into a new role that is a huge leap, losing a loved one through death or divorce, experiencing the birth of a child or grandchild, or being laid off from a job. During these significant emotional experiences, we reevaluate what is important to us, and we may shift our values hierarchy as a result.

Don, our 20-year-old marketing intern, has high Aesthetic and Social motivators. He is majoring in economics and entrepreneurship, although he shows no motivation in those directions. He may be building his ladder against the wrong wall for him to experience meaning and happiness in his work. It will be much harder for him to be successful in economics with these top motivators. As his coach or manager, your helping Don to realize this early on would be a huge gift to him. He will not be a star performer in an economics position. I learned in conversation with him that he majored in economics because that is what his father told him to do—Don's own passion was squashed. When asked about his passions, he described in great detail taking photographs for a Peace Corps project and his desire to create a new line of beers.

Workplace motivators also point to the topics on which people would be willing to focus their developmental efforts. For example, someone with a high Utilitarian value will enjoy focusing on entrepreneurial activities and making money. Someone with a low Utilitarian value would be turned off by that direction. If you want to get people passionately interested in their own career development path, you've got to connect to their top values.

Putting It into Action: Values

Andrew Cohn, an executive coach with The Professional Development Group, shared the following story about coaching an executive to understand the impact of his values on his leadership style and team dynamics.

Richard is the executive director of a nonprofit mental health organization. He is a very large, athletic man who could be physically imposing if his communication style were different. Richard is an extremely sensitive, compassionate man with high Social values. His leadership style was largely based on being helpful, supportive, and nurturing of his staff, who worked under very demanding circumstances. His values matched the core mission of the work they were involved in, which included counseling and physically caring for mentally ill residents while earning very minimal pay. For the most part, the staff members worked there because they believed in the mission of the organization (high Social values), not because the money was great (low Utilitarian values).

Richard had the wisdom to have an assistant, Paula, who was very detail oriented and tactical. She loved to solve problems using facts, data, and logic, which covered Richard's blind spots. When Andrew met with the two of them, Richard explained that his leadership was motivated by Social values, or "heart-based" values, and Paula was more motivated by Theoretical and Utilitarian, or "head-based" values. She would state the procedural steps that needed to be followed and would measure the results. He would be like a parent to the staff, nurturing them when they had personal challenges. This felt like a good cop–bad cop game to the staff. In this arrangement, Richard would let discipline and accountability slide because he was being too compassionate and putting all his passion into the Social motivator. For example, he would not challenge employees who were late or who submitted reports that were substandard because of problems they were having at home. He was not holding people accountable to the Job Benchmark because he wanted to be supportive and nice. Paula had to step in and hold the staff accountable.

A meaningful turning point in the coaching occurred when Richard clearly "got" a coaching point: it is critically important for leaders with high Social motivation to separate the employees' situations and behaviors from the employees. Andrew reminded Richard that his job as the executive director was to hold people accountable to performance standards and that doing so did not diminish the level of caring he may have for them as individuals. "It is not the whole person that you as the manager are responsible for guiding; it's the person's performance on the job. Focus on job behavior." Richard and Paula thanked Andrew repeatedly for that insight. For Richard, the key was Andrew's speaking to job performance—Richard's responsibility as a manager—that unlocked his most important value and how best to use it as a leader. When he shared this new insight with the team, they all understood and expressed their appreciation for Richard as a leader who could now keep his heart in his work without "losing his head."

Summary

It is much easier to connect with people, companies, and situations that will build momentum and growth when we are clear about who we really are. That is self-awareness. When we choose coaches, clients, bosses, career paths, and organizations that align with our top values, we have the best chance of offering what we naturally bring to the table and, hence, are provided with good opportunities to become star performers.

Phrases for Starting a Conversation
for Identifying Personal Motivators

- Who inspires you and why?
- What about your current work makes you feel most alive and passionate about being here?
- What do you appreciate about the team?
- When you consider how you have spent your time and money over the past several months, what do you notice about how it reflects your values?
- When I took the time to really understand my own motivators and why I do what I do, it helped me to make decisions about the projects I signed up for and the career path that would bring me the most fulfillment. I did this myself by (*share your steps here*), and I encourage you to do the same.
- In past roles, what caused you to be motivated?
- When you think about the next year and what we have on our to-do lists, what gets you jazzed up and excited?

Conversations for Identifying What Your Team Members Do Well

Being focused on strengths when developing others means that you clearly understand what they do well and that you create assignments that play to those abilities. It does not mean that you ignore their weaknesses or blind spots.

When hiring or inheriting new team members, it's important to discuss their strengths, development areas, and blind spots during the interview process. However, it's also important to ask questions like these in order to uncover their capabilities and determine what it will take for them to become star performers:

- Which of your skills do you most enjoy using?
- How do you imagine you will add value to our team?
- What types of assignments would most appeal to you?
- Would you give me some examples of projects you've worked on in the past that you were passionate about?
- How would you describe your communication style?
- What motivates you?

- What are your development areas—that is, skills you know you will need to develop in order to perform well in this position?
- What are you looking for from a manager?
- What did you appreciate most about your previous manager?

If you inherit new team members or a whole new team, ask similar questions in one of your early meetings. Explain that you prefer to play to people's strengths, to get to know them well, and that to do so, you'll need a solid understanding of each team member. Indicate that you want them to interview you too. Encourage questions about you and your background. It is as important for your new team members to understand your strengths as it is for you to understand theirs. You want team members who are willing and able to cover your blind spots too. After all, no one can be all things to all people—when we try to do so, we burn ourselves out.

The Importance of Feedback: Nancy

When coaching clients, I perform a perceptual 360-degree interview to get feedback about the people I am coaching from their bosses, peers, and employees. From this, I produce an anonymous report that does not quote any one person directly but summarizes all the feedback I hear from the survey and the conversations I have. Strengths, developmental areas, and blind spots become very clear from this feedback. Inevitably, the people I am coaching are a bit nervous about hearing the comments they have received from others. Most of the time people think the feedback will be much worse than it is. Surprised at the list of strengths and ways in which they add value, these coaching clients often feel more confident about their abilities after we have discussed the feedback. The report helps us to see exactly where others believe the investment in their development needs to focus.

Perhaps you recall Nancy from the Introduction? This feedback process made a big difference for Nancy and her ability to be seen as the star she already was in her new organization.

Six months earlier, a global company known as the world leader in its industry had hired Nancy as a director of marketing. While she aspired to be the best, Nancy's high standards for herself and her team members were causing trouble for her in building relationships with peers. They saw her as a change agent bringing in loads of unwanted, creative, new ideas to make busywork by replacing processes that had been working just fine. Her peers were ready for Nancy to go back to where she had come from when Nancy reached out to me and asked for coaching. She wanted to turn things around quickly, but she did not know how. This high-performing star was asking to develop her own interpersonal relationship building abilities, since this appeared to be the missing piece of her puzzle. Nancy's question was about how she might go about building strong relationships with peers and team members.

The perceptual interview feedback report helped Nancy to see clearly where we wanted to focus our developmental conversations. This is the feedback that was in her report:

Summary of Nancy's Strengths
- She has a strong executive presence.
- She makes a great presentation delivery.
- She creates tactics to attain higher levels of performance.
- She adds value to the team by offering her opinions and adding meaningful content to the conversation.
- In meetings, her comments add value and direction.
- I am confident to put her at the table with other business leaders because she is so articulate and thinks quickly.
- She makes decisions in a crisis.
- She is strong willed.
- She is a natural leader.
- She sets team goals and works with each team member to meet the goals.

- She has great passion and energy for her area of focus.
- She is comfortable speaking to people at all levels of the organization.
- She builds relationships with senior leaders.
- She gets to the real issues quickly.
- She has great financial acumen.
- She is dedicated to her work.
- She shares her expertise openly.

Summary of Nancy's Developmental Areas

Here is the plan I prescribed for Nancy, consisting of activities and behavior to do more of, and some to stop. This plan was based on the feedback from the people she included in the 360-degree perceptual interview process.

What to Do More Of

- *Listening:* She pushes her own agenda too often. Instead, she could listen and repeat or summarize what she heard and then add her opinions—say, "Let me think about what you have said, and I will get back to you after I've considered these ideas."
- *Flexibility:* She comes across as if there is a right way (hers) and a wrong way and nothing in between. She has strong views on what is wrong here, and she needs to realize that her views do not cause people to feel liked or appreciated.
- *Engaging:* She needs to reach out to understand more of the inputs to her work. To do this, she could invite her peers to collaborate by asking, "What are the top goals you are pushing for this year? What are you thinking of the role my team could play? How do you anticipate you would like support from us?"
- *Respectfulness:* She needs to express consideration, appreciation, and respect for what came before her. She needs to seek to understand how and why things were done the way they were before she arrived.
- *Approachability:* She needs to be friendlier toward others.

What to Do Less Of

- She needs to be less defensive. Some people feel nervous when working with her because she reacts physically when she does not like something or she disagrees with someone. She rolls her eyes and appears critical of others.
- When she notices that she has strong differing opinions or is not interested, she needs to be aware of her own body language.
- Her peers know she is gifted and driven. She does not have to prove that in every meeting. Her peers trust her, so she can be less defensive when she is trying to prove her point.
- She should not preface her comments with "My expertise and past experience suggest . . ." She needs to earn the right to say what she wants to say by being one of the team members who understands the culture and people's needs. She needs to base her opinions and remarks on the business facts as they are currently here—not as they were in her past experience in another company.

It was clear that Nancy's boss sees her as a star, and others will also, when she tweaks a few things about the way she interacts with her peers. I began the coaching sessions with Nancy asking her to look at where she could add value using the strengths others already see in her.

Raising Nancy's Self-Awareness

The developmental side of the conversation focused on helping her to raise her own awareness of when she could listen more actively. "Nancy, can you imagine yourself in a meeting listening by summarizing what you have heard, especially if it is complex or emotional in nature? Can you see yourself asking several sincere questions to gain more understanding, not to put the other person on the spot? Would you be willing to take these two steps before you share your own opinions and reactions?" As our conversations evolved, Nancy was practicing what I was suggesting to her in our discussion. I asked her to come to our coaching meeting the following week with at least three examples of times when she actively and deeply listened to another person or to team members.

The following week, Nancy and I began our conversation with those examples of situations in which she was able to practice. Nancy pulled out her learning journal and began. "I used the three steps of active listening by first paying attention to my own body language and summarizing in my own words what I had heard. Then I asked at least three questions that showed I was engaged, blending what I knew about the topic with my interest in hearing the others' points of view. Then I shared my opinion and/or reactions."

Nancy shared specific situations that had been complex or emotional and how she had caught herself and remembered to use active listening.

"Nancy, I can tell you have the ability to listen actively," I told her. "Now you'll want to keep practicing this intentionally until it becomes so automatic that you do it without thinking about it."

Somewhere along the way, my coaching clients will usually ask how long a certain skill takes to learn. The reality is that most of the time it will take at least 30 days of repeated practice to learn a new skill or break a habitual way of doing something. Remember when you learned how to drive a car? It took you many times to get to the point where you did not have to deeply concentrate to get it right, yes? The same will be true here.

By asking Nancy if she wanted to add another area of focus or if she'd prefer to stay focused on integrating the deep listening skill before moving on, I let her determine how long it would take for her. She was able to base the time on her schedule and the events going on before putting another developmental area on her plate. By giving her the choice, I allowed her to be the predominant creative force in our agenda setting. It is vital for people who are being coached to feel that they have a say in the agenda and focus.

Nancy indicated that she was ready to move on right then. Using the agenda we had established for developing new skills, her flexibility was the area for us to focus on next. We got right to it. I asked, "What does being flexible mean to you? Nancy, whom do you know who is flexible in a good way? What does that look like? Whom do you know who is flexible in a bad way? What does that look like? When you read the feedback that said people want more flexibility from you—'She comes across as if there is a right way (hers) and a wrong way and nothing in between'; 'She has such strong views on what is wrong here, and she needs to realize that her views do not cause people to feel liked or appreciated'—did you recognize it as feedback you had heard before?"

As I asked nonjudgmental questions about her flexibility, Nancy's awareness began to increase. I asked her to observe flexibility over the next two weeks and to write in her learning journal about what she notices when people are flexible both in a good way and in a way that does not serve them. I ended the session by acknowledging Nancy for the great job on deep listening and by summarizing again, with encouragement, that she should watch for evidence of flexibility in conversations with others during the next week. *Her assignment*: Come to our session with observations about your flexibility and where the line is between being too flexible and not flexible enough when deeply listening to others.

Hopefully, you are observing that this coaching conversation is specific to Nancy's feedback and will tie into her goals to be a star performer in her current role. This is a typical coaching conversation focused on developing Nancy in the areas that are her biggest needs if she is to be seen by others as the star performer she is capable of being.

Summary

Phrases for Starting a Conversation for Identifying "What You Do Well"

- Which skills or capabilities do you think you have fully developed already?

- What skills did you intentionally focus on developing in the past?
- How did you go about developing those capabilities?
- When you look at the key accountabilities for your role, which ones do you think you will want assistance with?
- Developmental areas are the skills and capabilities we want to develop in ourselves. It is best to focus on one or maybe two at a time. When you think about your key accountabilities, which areas do you think will be most important for you to focus on during the next 60 days?
- Blind spots are areas in which we realize it would be very hard for us to develop capabilities. It may be better to delegate those to someone else. When you reflect on your accountabilities, are there any areas where you realize you have a bind spot?

Stephanie Trotter, the director of leadership development at a major pharmaceutical company, said she believes, "It is vital to align people's roles so they are using their natural talents in the work they are doing." Stephanie, I agree and that's a perfect summary for this chapter.

Conversations for Creating Development Plans

Let's take a look at some of the different plans you can use to help your employees work on their strengths and blind spots.

The Importance of Individual Development Plans

Creating Individual Development Plans (IDPs) says we care enough about our employees to focus time on developing them for the future. It is a signal that we are making an investment for the long term. It has the potential to trigger hope and new possibilities and engage people in taking ownership for their future.

A Performance Improvement Plan (PIP) is another thing altogether. It says there is a problem with your current performance and something needs to be fixed in order for you to continue in the role you are in. No one wants a PIP. It triggers fear and anger in employees as they feel the need to defend their actions and document their experiences, and they often become mistrustful of their managers.

Many organizations need PIPs for a variety of reasons, primarily related to having someone whose performance is subpar and needing to document that effort was taken to help the employee perform up to expected standards. We are not focusing on PIPs here; however, I wanted to take a moment to explain the difference between the two.

A PIP is often a red flag waving to the employee that it is time to look for another job because the fit with the current one is not right. Many organizations have a 1-to-5 performance rating scale. In several organizations I work with, 5 is the highest rating and 1 is the lowest rating, and people in the 1 or 2 category have to be given a PIP. These organizations want to weed out the people who do not fit into their culture and role.

The Importance of Continuous Learning

Continuous learning is a way of life for successful businesspeople. No one has all the answers or is perfect all the time. Thus, there is value in continuing to learn. Having the spirit of an adventurer, ready to explore ways that will enable growth to the next level, creates momentum and makes life and work more interesting and fun.

Employee development plans begin with the employees' short-term and perhaps long-term goals. Relate these to the needs of the current role they are in and then perhaps to the roles they would like to grow into.

Brian Tracy has shared one of his greatest discoveries: "Your weakest key skill sets the height of your income and your success. You can make more progress by going to work on the one skill that is holding you back more than any other. The Key Question to ask is, 'What one skill, if you developed and did it in an excellent fashion, would have the greatest positive impact on your life?'"

If that skill is in your blind spot, could you put someone on your team or your personal board of advisors who has the ability and is willing to help you with it? Be aware of your weakest skills and abilities so they do not derail you.

Communication Style as a Clue to Where to Begin

What do you want to develop? It may already be clear to you where you want to focus. Many people I work with need awareness and perspective about the areas that at some point they will need to focus on developing.

There are several foreseeable areas in which the various types of employees will need to raise their awareness. What I mean is that based on their preferred communication styles and values, there are clear areas in which people will need to be aware that they could be derailed because of a potential weakness. Let's begin by looking at the developmental areas that naturally come from the strengths of each communication style. There are four core communication styles, each accompanied by developmental areas that align with that communication style.

Compliant-to-Standards Communication Style

People with this communication style usually demonstrate this cluster of strengths and behaviors:

- Analytical
- Conservative
- Focused on facts
- Careful
- Cautious
- Dependable
- Restrained
- Mature
- Accurate
- Conscientious
- Evasive
- Sensitive and deliberate

They do not like being loud or giddy, and they do not like to be pushed with unrealistic deadlines.

**Keys to Developing People with
a High Compliant-to-Standards Communication Style**

- Provide time to think before decisions are made.
- Provide your process and procedures in writing.
- Do not create sudden or abrupt changes.
- Involve them in defining and implementing the standards.
- Involve them in long-term planning.
- Allow them to work with a small group of people in a less verbal manner.
- Do not criticize their work unless you can demonstrate with proof that there is a better way of doing it.

They will likely have developmental needs that include these:

- Learning how to express their feelings and listen openly to others who are expressing themselves.
- Learning to be warm and friendly and willing to engage personally.
- Learning how to sell their ideas to gain buy-in.
- Learning not to be too critical, judgmental, or too harsh on others.
- Identifying when they are responding defensively and instead need to listen.
- Making decisions with the information they have rather than waiting for all the data to be produced; not overanalyzing.
- Learning about communication styles so they are able to understand the impact their style has on others.
- Learning to apologize and move on rather than building resentments.

If you have people with a high Compliant-to-Standards Communication Style on your team, help them to raise their own awareness about the strengths and blind spots that are natural with this style. Consider sharing this information with them and asking them to select one of the above areas to focus on. For example, if a person selects "Identifying when others perceive me to be responding defensively and instead listening," you can use the information in the Appendix on building listening skills to provide direction and support.

You'll also find helpful information in these sections of the Appendix:

1. Empathy
2. Emotional intelligence
3. Interpersonal skills
4. Persuasion
5. Teamwork
6. Conflict management

Steady Communication Style

People with this communication style usually demonstrate this cluster of strengths and behaviors:

- Steady
- Relaxed
- Modest
- Patient
- Listen to what is being said
- Reliable
- Systematic
- Dependable team players
- Introverted and methodical

They do not like being rushed into business, they are not domineering or demanding, and they do not like making quick decisions.

Keys to Developing People with a High Steady Communication Style

- Provide upcoming changes and prepare well in advance.

- Involve them in long-term planning.
- Ask "How?" questions.
- Allow them to complete what they begin.
- Assign them to work with a small group of people.
- Do not switch them from team to team frequently.
- Provide opportunities for creating harmony between home and work life.

High Steady Style communicators will likely have developmental needs that include these:

- Learning how to move through change because they can be highly resistant and cling to the past.
- Learning how to set personal goals and establish priorities.
- Taking initiative because they can be too passive or unclear about their own goals. They have a tendency to wait for orders before taking action.
- Learning how to speak up when they do not agree because they may have a tendency to give a false sense of agreement and then become resentful later.
- Showing a sense of urgency for the most important aspects of the project.
- Possibly needing a nudge when it is time for them to grow to the next level.

If you have people with a high Steady Communication Style on your team, help them to raise their own awareness about the strengths and blind spots that are natural to this style. Consider sharing this information with them and asking them to select one of the above areas to focus on. For example, if a person selects "Learning how to set personal goals and establish priorities," you can use the information in the "Goal Achievement" section of the Appendix to help him set his own goals and establish his priorities.

You'll also find helpful information in these sections of the Appendix:

1. Conflict management
2. Decision making
3. Flexibility
4. Goal achievement
5. Leadership
6. Negotiation

Dominant Communication Style

People with this communication style usually demonstrate this cluster of strengths and behaviors:

- Decisive
- Independent
- Goal oriented
- Strong-willed
- Ambitious
- Have a clear agenda
- Forceful
- Direct
- Challenging
- Have a strong desire to win
- Willing to take risks
- Juggle many balls at one time
- Highly energetic
- Can be outgoing when needed
- Self-starters

They do not like talking about things that are irrelevant to the issue, nor do they like to appear disorganized.

Keys to Developing People with a High Dominant Communication Style

- Provide challenges with new and varied experiences.
- Maintain their focus on the bottom line.
- Ask them to make decisions. Provide them options instead of directives.

71

- Ask them "What?" questions.
- Explain the results expected and the big picture.
- Define the rules up front because they will test the boundaries.

Dominant Style communicators will likely have developmental needs that include these:

- Learning to listen to others who are not as direct as they are.
- Learning not to be too blunt; knowing when and how to use tact and diplomacy in conversations.
- Understanding that other people are not as interested in challenges and quick decision making as they are.
- Learning to be solutions focused and not expressing frustration and anger as directly as they may naturally want to, especially with people who have a communication style different from theirs.
- Learning how to match their emotional intensity to fit the situation. Understanding that other people may be walking on eggshells, afraid that the Dominant Style communicator will be frustrated or angry again soon.
- Learning how to pace themselves and take time to relax. They may have a tendency to be workaholics, and they may burn themselves out physically without realizing they are doing so.
- Learning how to lead people rather than pushing them. Learning to let others win too.
- Learning the benefits of long-term relationship building. Understanding that when they focus too intensely on tasks and not enough on relationship building, they are hurting themselves.
- Learning how to set realistic project plans and goals for themselves and their own teams. They have a tendency to take on too many assignments too quickly, and if they are not aware of this, they will quickly burn out their team members and peers.

CONVERSATIONS FOR CREATING DEVELOPMENT PLANS

- Learning the importance of deep listening skills. They may need to be shown how to transition into listening when they might otherwise be argumentative and impatient with others.
- Learning the importance of collaborative leadership as opposed to pushing or demanding.
- Understanding that they have a tendency to overstep authority. Dominant Style communicators may need their leaders to provide clear boundaries so that they are able to create results within the norms and guidelines of the company.

You'll also find helpful information in these sections of the Appendix:

1. Diplomacy and tact
2. Emotional intelligence
3. Empathy
4. Interpersonal skills
5. Teamwork
6. Flexibility

Influential Communication Style

People with this communication style usually demonstrate this cluster of strengths and behaviors:

- Expressive
- Enthusiastic
- Friendly
- Outgoing
- Demonstrative
- Aware of the interpersonal dynamics
- Appreciate opportunities to discuss their feelings and are motivated by their gut reaction
- Persuasive
- Spontaneous

- Confident
- Open-minded
- Trusting
- Charming
- Inspiring
- Sociable

They do not like talking with people who are curt or cold, and they avoid analytical details and research.

Keys to Developing People with a High Influential Communication Style

- Look for opportunities for them to use their verbal skills and deliver presentations.
- Have an open-door policy with them, as they may need to verbalize their thinking in order to move forward.
- Be friendly and warm; connect on an emotional level.
- Help them to understand that they are verbal learners and information processors and that they will need much more time to talk and discuss than do people who have the other styles. Guide them to use a journal and to be in a regular conversation with themselves in the journal.
- People with this communication style need praise and acknowledgment more often than you may realize.

Influential Style communicators will have developmental needs that include these:

- Managing time and establishing priorities.
- Setting realistic goals.
- Organizing their space and systems.
- Learning when they are overselling their ideas or talking too much.
- Learning when they are being impulsive and too emotional.
- Identifying when they are trusting people indiscriminately.

- Identifying when they are being inattentive to details that are important to their work.
- Realizing that they have a tendency to overdelegate and underinstruct.

You'll also find helpful information in these sections of the Appendix:

1. Planning and organizing
2. Goal achievement
3. Self management
4. Emotional intelligence
5. Resiliency

Workplace Motivators as Revealing Developmental Areas

We've explored how communication styles impact developmental needs. Because of the strength of the style, when a strength is overused, it can sometimes become a blind spot that the person being developed needs to be aware of. Learning where the fine line is between a strength that is being used well and a strength that is being overused and thus becoming a blind spot requires feedback from others.

Our workplace motivators also provide clues to the ways in which we add value to teams as well as where our developmental needs will likely bubble up. We discussed this phenomenon in Chapter 3 in the situation in which Richard became aware of the impact of his high Social values on his team. Now let's explore each of the motivators—Theoretical, Utilitarian, Traditional, Social, Individualistic, and Aesthetic—and how they impact our developmental needs.

A person with high Theoretical motivators—wanting opportunities to learn, answers, facts, data, and truth and to share knowledge—may have developmental areas including these:

- They may use theory too much without making it actionable for others.
- Their pursuit of knowledge may be so intense that they ignore or neglect practical matters.
- They may put their personal safety at risk to discover the truth.
- They need to learn to appreciate emotions and the expression of subjective experiences with no rational justification.

A person with high Utilitarian motivators—wanting things to be useful and productive, seeking financial well-being, and possibly using money or points to keep the score focused on practicality and return on investment—may have developmental areas including these:

- They need to learn how to balance work and personal life. They may be workaholics who burn out physically.
- They may focus too intensely on self-preservation and demonstrate little concern for or interest in others around them who want their support.
- They may become overfocused on saving resources, time, materials, and services.

A person with high Traditional motivators—wanting instructions or procedures so that life can be lived or work can be done correctly—may have developmental areas including these:

- They may be close-minded and judgmental of others and not willing to listen to people who do not share their beliefs.
- They may sacrifice themselves for their beliefs—being so intense or extreme in their beliefs that they are willing to die for them.
- They may break the rules or the law to follow their closed "book" of how things should be.

A person with high Social motivators—wanting to make a difference for others; wanting to solve people issues such as hate, poverty, homelessness, and hunger; and wanting to address political issues—may have developmental areas including these:

- They need to beware of taking on other people's personal problems as their own.
- They are apt to be overzealous for a cause, which may lead to harmful behavior for themselves and others.
- They may believe it is all on their shoulders to solve complex people problems. They may give away all of their time, money, or resources to do so without seeing the impact on their own future.

A person with high Individualistic motivators—wanting to be victorious at the table when decisions are made, seeking to be a leader whose voice matters, winning and leading in a world-class way—may have these developmental areas:

- They may demand promotions and advancement when they have not yet paid the price to earn them.
- They may want to work only on the best projects or with the senior team.
- They may dominate others so that they can be the leader.
- They may be corrupted by or overfocused on the power of their position.

A person with high Aesthetic motivators—wanting things to feel good, look good, or sound pleasing, and being artistic, creative, and highly subjective—may have the following developmental areas:

- They may be overly disturbed when someone does not appreciate the form, beauty, and harmony in self, others, and the environment.

- They may need to learn to operate in current reality and look at, rather than dismiss the current data, trends, and facts.

Individual Development Plans

So far we've discussed communication styles and workplace motivators and the natural areas for development that come about as a result of the strengths of each is foundational. These will be areas in which individuals will need to stay aware of their natural limitations. It may take months or years to resolve these natural developmental issues so that they can be highly effective star performers.

It is useful for star performers to have their own unique professional developmental plan.

What Is Included in Individual Development Plans?

There is no one right format for Individual Development Plans. The most important point is that development plans be clearly unique to the individuals' current needs for the role they are in now and possibly the role they are developing for. Each part of the development plan speaks to what is now (the current role) and where the growth opportunities are for future roles. Have you ever sat through a training program as an attendee, even though you had enough expertise in the topic to be leading the training? This is what sometimes happens when managers assign employees to attend training that is not related to their current developmental areas within a strategic big picture. Time and money are wasted when coaching and training aren't customized to each individual's needs. Sophisticated talent management systems now offer options that hone in on the competencies needed for the current or future position based on a strategic talent plan.

I am sharing what we include when we create a Personalized Job-Related Development Plan as the foundation for development. I suggest giving employees and coaching clients their own unique plan that contains these sections:

- Job Benchmark that shows the key accountabilities and what is needed for success in the role
- Unique Talent Report that shows the employee's competencies hierarchy, motivators, behavioral hierarchy, summary of competencies, and dimensional balance
- Gap Report that highlights where the job and the person are aligned and where there are gaps today
- Coaching Report that helps the employee to understand his or her own preferred communication style, workplace motivators, acumen and competencies, and emotional intelligence patterns
- Action Plan that ties all the parts together with direction about where to focus our developmental conversations, including action steps in priority order

The first four parts of the Personalized Job-Related Development Plan build awareness of current expectations and competencies. They lead up to the most important part of the plan—the Action Plan—which gives focus for the ongoing coaching.

Most organizations I work with use the Princeton University Learning Process, 70/20/10 Model. The model is a learning and development formula based on research that has found that 70 percent of learning and development takes place from real-life and on-the-job experiences, tasks, and problem solving. This is the most important aspect of any learning and development plan. For example, the real learning from a skill acquired in a training program, or from feedback, takes place back on the job when the skill or feedback is applied to a real situation. Another 20 percent comes from feedback and from observing and working with role models. Then 10 percent comes from formal training like attending a workshop or reading a book.

For me, the model is more meaningful when I reorder the list: spend 10 percent of your time in coaching or training that focuses you on the specific areas to learn, then 20 percent of your time observing people who are experts at what you are learning, and 70 percent of your time applying what you have learned so you become masterful at executing the ability. Once you have become masterful in one capability, select another one from your Individual Development Plan. This is continuous learning.

Let me point out a nuance that sometimes gets lost when people look at this in the 70/20/10 order. When you learn a new model or a new way of doing something, track how much time it takes you to understand the model. Consider that to be the 10 percent in this formula. Now multiply that times 20 percent, and spend that much time doing it with an expert who can give you feedback on how you are doing. Then multiply your original number by 70 percent and allocate that much time to practicing the new ability before you take on another new learning goal.

In the action planning phase, we work together to identify specific assignments, work projects, and real-life experiences that will enable the coachee to practice the skills we are focused on.

Who Creates or Writes Individual Development Plans?

Ideally, these documents are joint efforts that include input from the manager and/or coach and the employee. The Job Benchmark requires that the boss be involved in providing input on the expectations of the role. The employee needs to reflect on this and help to establish the Action Plan. Ultimately, the employee being coached owns the outcomes of the development plan. When employees are brand-new in a role, they may not have the awareness to design their first 90-day development plan. Their mangers may need to do that for them. After the 90-day period is over, however, the development planning needs to be a joint effort to keep engagement high.

Beginning the Conversations for Creating Individual Development Plans

To introduce the idea of Individual Development Plans to your team, you could say something like the following:

> As you know, in our department *(or team or organization)*, we have a commitment to continuous learning. We've found that when people are focused on learning, they are more likely to be creative in problem solving and sharing information with others. This creates a thriving culture. We want to foster more sharing of learning, and that is part of the reason why we have created the mentoring program and are intentionally building a continuous learning culture. Another thing that I want to do with each person in the department is to create an Individual Development Plan. I'll be talking with each of you one-on-one about your own unique plan. Please give some thought to areas in which you are interested in growing and developing professionally.

To introduce the idea of Individual Development Plans to a new employee, you could say something along these lines:

> Paolo, I think you have a great deal of potential. Because of your strengths in XYZ, I sense you could grow in your current role. Would that be of interest to you? If so, let's create an Individual Development Plan that focuses on what star performance in your role looks like.

Making Individual Development Plans Relevant and Easy

If you completed a Job Benchmark that shows the expectations of the role and had the employee complete a Talent Assessment showing where he or she is in each of the job dimensions, you could then provide a Coaching Report that focuses on the employee's current strengths and blind spots. In this case the development plan would be 100 percent relevant to the job and would be very easy to deliver to the employee. Here is an example of what you could say:

> Marco, we are thrilled to have you in your new role in the company! Because we see so much potential for you to be a star performer here, I wanted to provide you with an Individual Development Plan. Do you recall taking the assessments online? From that, we were able to compare your current ability level to the needs of your job and identify where the current gaps are. This report shows us together where we may want to focus our developmental energies to help you get up to speed in your new role. I'd like to schedule time together to discuss this Individual Development Plan. (*Yes, my office can help to provide this tool: www.TheProfessionalDevelopmentGroup.com.*)

Common areas of focus included in Individual Development Plans (sometimes also called Performance Development Plans):

- Volunteer projects that relate to developing skills on the job
- Working with or shadowing an expert
- Certifications desired and when they will be completed
- Assignments desired, such as serving on the organization's cross-functional branding project
- A milestone date for moving to the next level of performance
- Future roles, assignments, or opportunities to explore
- Desired training or workshops
- Desired coaching or mentoring support

Further Benefits of Individual Development Plans

One of my clients shared her IDP with me during our first meeting. It was organized into the following sections:

- Current strengths and competencies

- Short-term goals
- Long-term goals
- Areas of developmental focus
- Strategies for each developmental area
- Action Plan and timeline
- How results will be measured

After she shared her IDP, we discussed her career and her goals, and we got to know each other. We then completed a Job Benchmark for her current role to illuminate any gaps between where she is now and where she wants to be. This was very helpful, and she added that to her IDP also.

Creating an organizational culture that respects Individual Development Plans has many benefits:

- Brands your company as being interested in developing people—setting people up for success in their role, not failure
- Encourages employees to take responsibility for their career planning
- Encourages employees to learn from and with each other collaboratively
- Focuses employees on being lifetime learners, not lifetime employees

Ultimately, an organization's support for Individual Development Plans will lead to happy, growing employees, which will lead to happy, growing customers

Summary: Checklist of Developmental Areas

Are you looking for the best way to describe a developmental area but can't quite get it right? Here is a list of the most common ones that we've discussed in this chapter and some others as well. By including this list, my intent is to provide you with a useful resource when you are looking for just the right way to describe a developmental area you have observed in someone you are coaching.

- Learning how to sell ideas to gain buy-in and learning how to encourage others to care about your ideas
- Learning not to be too critical, too judgmental, or too harsh
- Learning to be warm and friendly and willing to engage personally
- Identifying when you are responding too defensively instead of listening
- Learning to express your feelings and listening openly to others who are expressing their feelings
- Making decisions with the information that is available now rather than waiting for all the data to be produced and then overanalyzing the data
- Gaining awareness about communication styles to influence others more effectively
- Learning to apologize and move on rather than holding resentments and bitterness
- Learning how to move through change instead of being highly resistant to change and clinging to the past
- Learning how to set goals and establish priorities for yourself and others
- Taking initiative instead of being too passive or unclear about your own goals
- Taking initiative instead of waiting for orders or direction from others
- Learning how to speak up when you do not agree (You may have a tendency to give a false sense of agreement and then become resentful later.)
- Showing a sense of urgency for the most important aspects of the project
- Listening to others who are not as direct as you are
- Learning not to be too blunt—that is, when to use tact and diplomacy in conversations

- Understanding that other people are not necessarily as interested in challenges and quick decision making as you are
- Being patient—not expressing frustration and anger as directly as you may naturally want to, especially with people who have a communication style different from yours
- Understanding that other people may be walking on eggshells in fear that you will be frustrated or angry again soon (You may need to learn how to match your emotional intensity to fit the situation.)
- Pacing yourself and taking time to relax (You may have a tendency to be a workaholic, and you may burn yourself out physically without realizing you are doing this.)
- Leading people rather than pushing or controlling them
- Learning to let others win too—celebrating others' accomplishments rather than being jealous or a poor sport when they win
- Learning to allocate time and establish priorities
- Learning to set realistic goals
- Learning how to organize paper, space, and systems
- Identifying when you are overselling ideas so you can shift gears to asking questions and listening
- Learning when you are being impulsive and too emotional, so you can pull back to thinking things through more comprehensively
- Evaluating other people's results, not just their words or looks
- Identifying when you are being inattentive to details that are important to your work so you can then refocus
- Learning to give clear directions and goals instead of overdelegating with too little guidance
- Being aware of practical matters when your pursuit of knowledge may be so intense that it is causing you to ignore or neglect them
- Appreciating the emotions and expression of subjective experiences with no rational justification, which can be

especially important when working with people who are very different from you

- Learning how to balance your work and personal life (You may be a workaholic who burns out physically.)
- Showing concern for others (You may focus too intensely on self-preservation and demonstrate little concern or interest in others around you who want or need your support.)
- Releasing hoarding (You may become overfocused on saving resources, time, materials, and services.)
- Learning to listen deeply instead of being judgmental of others and unwilling to listen to people who do not share your beliefs
- Being aware when you are taking on someone else's personal problems as your own
- Being overzealous for a cause that may lead to harmful behavior for yourself and others
- Believing it is all on your shoulders to solve complex people problems and giving away all of your time, money, or resources to do so without seeing the impact on your own future
- Demanding promotions and advancements when you have not yet paid the price to earn them
- Wanting to work only on the best projects or with the senior team
- Dominating others in an attempt to be the leader
- Being corrupted by or overfocused on the power of your position
- Needing to learn to operate in current reality

You will find specific language and action steps that you can use when creating a development plan in the next chapter and in the Appendix.

Conversations for Developing New Skills

Have you ever reflected on a simple conversation, perhaps with your boss, a peer, or one of your employees, and realized after the fact that you left the discussion knowing how to do something new that you did not know how to do before? If so, then what you experienced was a conversation for developing new skills. "Work your strengths" does not mean ignoring your blind spots. Playing to your strengths is smart business! However, your blind spots can derail you if you are not aware of them and how they impact your relationships.

Imagine you are eavesdropping on me while I am leading a workshop for a group of coaches and we are role-playing in front of the participants an example of how to set up this type of conversation with a coaching client. I'm sitting in a chair across from the volunteer coaching client—let's call him Sam. I look into Sam's eyes and I say something like this:

Sam, what one skill, if you went to work on it and were able to perform at a high level, would have the greatest positive impact on your career? When you think about your role models, the people who are doing what you really want to do, what skill have they developed that you have not yet developed? Whatever skill that is, it should be something you want to develop within yourself. After all, if your role model could learn the process, the step-by-step actions to take to accomplish results, you can do it too!

It may come as a surprise to learn that your weakest key skill determines the height of your success and income level. You will make more progress by focusing on developing the one skill that is holding you back more than any other. However, you have to be the one who decides to identify and develop your blind spots and weaknesses. It does not work when someone bullies or uses fear-based incentives to make you develop your weaknesses—that creates only resentment and bitterness. If you have developed your strengths and you are now on a plateau feeling stuck, you can decide for yourself to look in the mirror to really see what is holding you back. You can summon up the courage to focus on developing your weakness. It is your choice!

At this point I break out of the role-playing and turn to the audience of coaches. I ask them, "What do you think Sam is feeling now based on what I've said to him?" The coaches say he is likely feeling inspired to rethink his abilities. Sam jumps into the discussion and says, "Even though I know this is role-playing, I am in it. I am feeling excited to look at my weakness because I want to grow beyond where I am now." We all want to feel like we are growing. We want to experience forward movement and momentum that is meaningful to us individually and to the organizations in which we work.

Dealing with a Specific Competency

When it is clear which abilities need development, you will find this chapter very helpful in guiding the direction. If you are a coach or manager who is helping one of your performers to develop, or if you are looking for a blueprint for your own development, think of this chapter as providing a menu or framework for your coaching conversations related to developing these specific competencies. In addition, in the Appendix you will find a menu of the following 24 skill areas that you can use as a reference guide in developing the desired skills:

- Conceptual thinking
- Conflict management
- Continuous learning
- Creativity
- Customer focus
- Decision making
- Diplomacy and tact
- Emotional intelligence
- Empathy
- Employee development and coaching
- Flexibility
- Futuristic thinking
- Goal achievement
- Interpersonal skills
- Negotiation
- Persuasion
- Planning and organization
- Presenting
- Problem solving
- Resiliency
- Self-management
- Teamwork
- Written communication

Perhaps you have a competency model already created for your organization. If so, you will find that your competencies will map easily to the ones included here. If you want some help doing that, e-mail admin@TheProfessionalDevelopment Group.com or fax your organization's competency model to 888-959-1188 and we will help you match them to our model.

They Have to Want It

Once an employee or coaching client is saying, "I want to do a better job of _____," then you will be ready to dive into the specifics related to how to develop that skill. Until the person being coached asks for guidance in a specific area, he or she is not ready to go into this type of conversation. You may recall that I shared earlier that fixing people does not work.

This is the point in a conversation that determines if you are crossing a line with someone: if you begin to tell an adult how to develop a skill and he or she is not asking for that know-how, you have skipped over an important awareness building conversation. People being coached need to acknowledge and understand why it is important for them to develop the skill. If you are managing or coaching people, before you dive into the specifics, begin with the awareness building and capabilities conversations that we discussed previously in the book.

Do you recall Alex from the Introduction? He told me his goal was to lead his employee, Bob, to change his core communication style and preference about how he engages with other people, even though Bob had never expressed the desire to do this. Alex had gone into fix-it mode with Bob. Alex had crossed a line that would cause failure if he continued to pursue that goal. Alex had to change his expectations of what was possible in developing Bob as a performer in the role he was in. The fact was that Bob was not a good fit for the work that needed to be done, and no amount of pushing on Alex's part would change this. This is what I said to Alex:

> Alex, are you saying that you've set a goal to change Bob's core communication style and preferences about how he engages with other people, but Bob himself has not expressed this as a goal? And is your motive for doing this because you want your boss to view you as a strong leader?

Alex replied happily, "Yes! Shawn, you understand completely what I am doing."

I replied with a warm expression indicating no judgment in my tone or body language, and then I carefully explained the situation. We had to do some unpacking of Alex's thinking. There were two layers of influence in Alex's goal that were worth examining. If Bob had not expressed a desire to modify his communication style preferences to be better aligned to the work he is responsible for, asking him to do so when he did not see the connection would cause him significant stress. If Bob decided on his own that this was his goal, it would still take a great deal of focus and energy for him.

The second issue was that highly effective leadership is not about convincing people to change their natural core style, strengths, and abilities. Leadership is more about identifying the natural talents that are already there and playing to those, developing the potential that is there now, and moving those employees into roles that need the talents they have.

We are viewed as effective leaders when we put the right people into the right roles, so there is a match between what the job naturally rewards as a result of the work that is being done in that role and what the employee brings to the table. I sensed that Alex wanted to make a square peg fit into a round hole. He wanted the first chair violinist to put down the violin and instead go play the piano. That would be very painful—even more painful than admitting that Bob was not the right fit for the role he was in. Why not help that square peg find a role that needs a square peg and then find a round peg for the work that needs to be done here?

Fixing people does not work. As he reflected on what we discussed, Alex evolved his own thinking and posed his new question for our coaching work together: how could he develop people based on who they were and put the right people into the right roles that will bring out their natural talents?

Developing Skills Takes Time

Recall that when you learned to drive, manage your finances, interview for a new job, or write monthly reports that your boss appreciated, these abilities did not materialize overnight. It took you weeks of practice and patience with yourself as you stumbled your way forward in accomplishing your goal. Today you may be masterful in these abilities. The same is true for developing any new skills.

First, we are *unconsciously incompetent*—we do not even know we do not know. "Blissful ignorance" is another name for this stage. When something or someone raises our awareness so that we want to know how to do it ourselves, we are *consciously incompetent*. This stage can be painful or feel like a challenge— we have questions about how to begin, what to do, and how to practice the right actions, behaviors, and thinking to achieve the desired results. As a coach or manager, you are facilitating this development process by asking questions and sharing guidance, experience, and direction at the time they are most helpful. You may be modeling or demonstrating exactly how to do it. Providing opportunities to practice repeatedly leads the employees to being at first *consciously competent* and later *unconsciously competent*.

Some skills or competencies will be easier for us to develop than others. What was something that was easy for you to learn to do? What was something that was easy for you but harder for someone else? Do you recall something that another person learned much more easily than you did?

I've observed that those people who have struggled to learn how to do something are often better teachers or coaches of that material than the people to whom it came naturally and who did not have to work at learning it. When people struggle to learn a new skill, they focus on each step. They practice over and over until they gain mastery. That practice becomes a gift in that these learners see distinctions in the skill development steps that others miss. These insights enable them to be better observers and to give clearer feedback to those they are coaching.

Raising Awareness of the Skill That Needs Developing

After clients have said they want to develop the XYZ ability, the first step coaches need to take is to raise their clients' awareness of that ability by asking questions like these:

- What is important about this ability to you?
- How will having this ability benefit you?
- Whom do you know who is particularly good at XYZ ability?
- What do they currently do differently than you do?
- How do they think about or approach XYZ?
- Is there anything you realize they do not do that you are currently doing?
- What else do you notice about XYZ?
- When is it useful to stop doing XYZ?

Let me give you an example of how this sounds when one of my coaching clients indicates that she wants to focus on developing presentation skills. Imagine I am coaching Isabella, who has recently been promoted to lead the sales department. She has been wildly successful at managing the customer service team, and now for the first time in her career she has to start delivering presentations on site at customer organizations in her new sales leader role:

Shawn: *Isabella, thank you for sharing with me that you are clear that you want to become a successful presenter so you can be a star in your new role. Whom do you know who is particularly good at presenting?*
Isabella: *Juan is a great presenter. He captures the audience's attention immediately by sharing a story or example that links to the topic.*
Shawn: *What else does Juan do that causes him to be a presenter you admire?*

93

Isabella: *He knows his material so well that he can take questions at any time without being nervous. I guess that is because he has practiced so much.*

Shawn: *How do you think Juan approaches preparing for a presentation? What does he think about and practice as part of his preparation?*

Isabella: *Hmm, I never thought about that. Juan probably thinks about who is going to be in the audience and what they need to know. He always seems to be prepared for any type of question that will be asked, but he has probably thought about what the audience is likely to be questioning. He also has an agenda that he has prepared in advance. He stays with his agenda for the most part, but at the same time he is also flexible enough that he can move off of it if the audience changes focus.*

Shawn: *Is there anything you think that Juan does not do in preparing for or delivering a presentation?*

Isabella: *Well, I've never heard Juan use filler words like um, uh, ahh, or okay. He also does not look nervous because he stands up straight and has eye contact with the person or group he is presenting to. That is something I really need to work on because I know I say um and okay too much when I am nervous.*

Shawn: *What else do you notice about people who are great presenters?*

Isabella: *They tell their own stories, not jokes that don't fit with the message or theme of the meeting. They have several stories they can use to connect with the audience, and they rotate from facts and data to stories and examples.*

Shawn: *Those are great observations, Isabella. I agree with you. When is the right time to stop the presentation, and what do great presenters do when it is time to stop?*

Isabella: *Well, our sales meetings usually have a stop time, so it is vital that the presenters not overstay their welcome. It is better to be brief and to the point, and offer to take questions, than to be too long-winded or go into too much detail. Oh, also it is important to summarize the key points and any follow-up activities that have been agreed to.*

Shawn: *Isabella, would you be willing to practice doing the things you've described during the next week? Will you put together a sample presentation and deliver it for me next week so we can observe what you are doing well and where you may need to make some adjustments in your delivery? I'd like to videotape you so that we can watch together to see what else you would like to focus on as you develop your presentation ability, okay?*

That example can be applied to **any** competency when you are coaching employees and trying to raise their awareness. In follow-up conversations, it will be important to provide employees with opportunities to practice the specific, right actions, behaviors, and thinking that will lead to mastery of the skill. As a manager, you need to be clear on what the right actions, behaviors, and thinking are. Create a process or framework for the employees to use to develop the ability. When they do not know how to do something, they are looking to you to provide the specific next steps they need to take. It is also useful for you to share your own inspiring story about how you developed the skill yourself.

As a manager of star performers, you should have a step-by-step plan that shows people how to accomplish more and achieve proven results. You'll need to create a document that shows off your track record. Do you have a plan to give your employees that provides them certainty and confidence that if they take the steps you've listed, they will produce the desired results? If not, begin to do so now. Break it down into actionable chunks that are sequenced from beginning to end in a framework of understandable elements that lead to clear milestones and outcomes.

Ideas and action steps are the organizing pieces of your managing content. One of the distinguishing factors of success for world-class managers is the energy, enthusiasm, and optimistic confidence they have because they can share how to accomplish the desired results. Collect uplifting stories about people who have succeeded despite obstacles when developing the abilities you specialize in. Insert words and phrases that will help your employees feel inspired and believe in themselves. Here are a few to get you started:

- I have confidence in you because I have observed you doing XYZ and I know if you can do that, you can learn how to do this too!
- If you put your mind to it and stay focused on achieving the desired result, you are going to succeed!
- What was something difficult that you learned how to do in the past that now you do consistently well as a star performer? How did you learn how to do it? If you learned that, you can learn this too!
- If you have seen others do it, you can learn to do it too. It may take you time, but if you are committed enough, you will be able to learn how to do it too.

In the Appendix, you will find examples of the ways I talk about developing skills in the 24 areas listed. You'll find ideas on what to practice and what to look for and the thinking that generates growth in those specific competencies.

In the Appendix, I also suggest resources, books, and/or websites to give you direction for the 10 percent of your coaching time that focuses you on what to use as your coaching model. The people you are coaching need a trusted framework in which to learn specific skills. However, the time it takes them to learn the framework will be 10 percent of the equation to mastery. To jump-start your employees' learning, use the frameworks I've listed in the Appendix. This will determine what the 10 percent of the time to mastery number will be as they understand the framework for learning. Then you need to allocate 20 percent of the skill development time to your employees' getting expert feedback as they practice with people who are already star performers in the ability. Finally, you need to allocate 70 percent more time for your employees to practice the ability on their own. This is the pathway to mastery of any skill. And, it will work for any skills you would like to develop too.

Mastery begins with being a student. Congratulations on being here because you have made a commitment to your own mastery and to being the best in your field by continuing to learn. I respect you for being committed to mastery.

Summary

Continuously developing new skills and abilities is vital in professional careers. Your conversations with employees and coaches can trigger them to want to develop new skills. You'll want to hear the people you are focused on developing say for themselves "I want to be able to do XYZ" before you jump into teaching the steps involved.

You'll need to be inspiring and connect the dots to show why having the new ability will be beneficial. You will likely have to unpack some thinking that your employees or coachees currently have and put new beliefs and thinking in its place.

Guiding your aspiring star performers to identify a specific skill they want to develop is only part of the process. The other part is helping them raise their awareness of the skill by asking questions like these:

- What is important about this ability to you?
- How will having this ability benefit you?
- Whom do you know who is particularly good at XYZ ability?
- What do they currently do differently than you do?
- How do they think about or approach XYZ?
- Is there anything you realize that they do not do that you are currently doing?
- What else do you notice about XYZ?
- When is it useful to stop doing XYZ?

And, believe in your own ability to guide and inspire. By being a life-long learner yourself, you will have stories that you can share when you are developing people that will help build rapport and trust.

Conversations for Getting Back on Track

How do you become a world-class manager who is known for developing star performers? By mastering the conversations described in this book! Your content—the guidance and direction that you share that is actionable and enables the people you are developing to shorten their learning curve—shows up in conversations over time. Your ability to create meaningful conversations will set you apart from others.

Some of the most important conversations you will have with the people you are coaching will be the ones that help them through a point at which they are stuck. These types of conversations can help increase people's trust in us as well as their respect for us. Managers often have to deal with times when people have gotten off track. Sometimes we have to say, "This is not working, and it's time to create a new solution. Let's do it together."

Two Paths to Getting Back on Track

Two paths are possible here: The people we are developing know they are off track and therefore bring up the issue. Or the people we are developing are oblivious to the problem. You'll want to handle these two situations differently.

When the Employee Brings the Problem to Your Attention

If the person you are developing brings up a challenge he or she is facing and indicates feeling off track, he or she is demonstrating that there is safety and trust in your relationship. Ask these questions:

• Looking forward, what could be the best possible outcomes? List a few possibilities.
• Where do you want to go from here to move toward the best possibility?
• What do you really want to accomplish?
• What will you need to focus on for this to happen?
• What are the current obstacles you'll need to overcome to move in the right direction? What is the first step you will take to begin moving in the right direction?
• Who else could help you with this?

Your questions encourage new thinking and enable the person for whom you are being a sounding board to examine new ideas. After asking several of these questions, you can provide specific guidance and insight concerning actions, behaviors, and next steps that you realize will help get things back on track. Then acknowledge and thank the employee for bringing the issue up for discussion.

When the Employee Is Oblivious to the Problem

Let's take a look at the more challenging situation in which the person is seemingly oblivious to the issue. How can you help him or her to become aware of the problem without going into fix-it mode and triggering fear and anger? This requires a well-built emotional bank account—one in which many positive deposits have been made over time. In other words, it requires trust and that the person you are developing understands your motives and goodwill.

When momentum has been lost, how do you regain it? First, reconnect to the bigger goals or values that both of you share. If you know that she is motivated by strong Social and Theoretical values, you might find a way to encourage her to connect the dots to solve people problems in new ways or to learn about the underlying issues facing people and explore how she could use her research to be helpful.

There will be times when the people you are developing do not realize they are off track and need to make an adjustment to reach their goals. In these cases, they need specific feedback or guidance to recalibrate their actions. Directives that give a clear picture of the next action steps are useful to people who are stuck. A clear directive is something like, "Keep a time log in 15-minute increments starting immediately following our meeting, and track how you use your time during the next three days."

Linda Bishop, the senior vice president for specialty markets at MileStone Bank, says there are four reasons why people do not do what you want them to do. She shares this framework with every manager who works for her:

1. They do not know what you want them to do.
2. They do not know how to do it.
3. They do not want to do it.
4. They are incapable of doing it.

In a previous role, Linda had 225 people reporting to her. A large part of her responsibility was working with managers and helping them to develop their newly hired teams. Linda realized that managers can buy talent or they can train talent. It is more expensive up front to buy talent than it is to hire undeveloped people and train them. So she hired people with two years of experience with the intention of developing them. Here is how

Linda discussed each of these stages with the managers who were responsible for developing these new employees:

1. *The solution to employees or coachees **not knowing what you want them to do** is communication.* Talk through the role, clearly defining each action and the desired outcomes.

2. *The solution to employees or coachees **not knowing how to do it** is training that sets the foundation for their thinking and behaviors related to achieving the goal.* Show them how to do it and what the desired finished product looks like. Then provide development feedback day to day for the next 30 days as they practice obtaining the desired results themselves.

3. *The solution if employees or coachees **do not want to do it** is to have a motivation-focused conversation about their values and workplace motivators.* Talk through the positive and negative consequences for the individuals and for the organization of not doing it. Help them to make a conscious decision about their own motivation for the task that is needed. Highlight the rewards that come from the nature of the work itself.

4. *The solution if employees or coachees **are incapable of doing it** is to have them clearly see that this is a job mismatch—that it is trying to put a square peg in a round hole.* You will not know if someone is incapable until you have ensured that possibilities 1 through 3 were covered. Once you know for sure that these possibilities have been covered, the people being coached themselves will understand what they need to do to move into another role that is a better fit for their strengths and current capabilities.

The value in learning how to get people unstuck and back on track is worth its weight in gold. You serve a very specific purpose for the people you are developing. Your role as an expert coach is to inspire and instruct others to achieve their goals and improve their lives. If you do not inspire them to get unstuck and have clarity about the next steps to take to get on the right track, you are not fulfilling your role as a star coach. Become an inspiration to other people to achieve what they want to achieve. Reignite in yourself and others the passion to grow and to move forward.

I worked in an organization that had a strategy to develop talent by hiring college graduates with one to three years of experience. Our goal was to inspire them to be world-class star performers in customer support. We trained them to fit into our culture and to do the job in a way that exceeded the expectations of our customers. This created great momentum and an exciting learning culture. The organization won awards for the career path and development programs that we created. At the end of the third year of doing this, there was a well-developed talent pool in place and numerous awards in the lobby showcasing their accomplishments.

Then the senior leadership changed, and with it the strategy shifted to focus more on buying talent at higher levels instead of developing from within. This shift created a significant change in the values of the culture. Those people who were engaged in being part of a learning organization now felt squashed. When these types of culture changes occur, they can also trigger the need for a conversation focused on recalibrating and getting back on track with the current focus of the organization. Sometimes people have to acknowledge that the organization has changed and is no longer the right fit for them or that they need to recalibrate their own goals because of the organization's shift. For these shifts in direction to succeed, inspiration from a coach who is committed to being a guide for world-class results helps.

Giving Difficult Feedback by Putting It in Context

Juan received feedback from Kristi, his manager, saying that he needed to "do a better job of communicating with the staff." That was it. With frustration in her voice, Kristi said this immediately after a team meeting as she and Juan walked out together.

In the hallway, with other people passing by, Kristi spoke curtly and then turned and walked away. Because of the way Kristi communicated her message to Juan, he spent a great deal of time wondering if he was about to lose his job or be put on a Performance Improvement Plan. He did not sleep well that night, and he worried that HR would be calling him into their office. He did not understand the context of the feedback, and therefore, he did not see his own next area for developmental focus. Because she did not put any context around the feedback, Kristi triggered fear in Juan instead of an understanding of what action steps to take and why.

In a private one-on-one conversation, Kristi would have made a better impact if she had spoken about the circumstances leading up to the moment, like this: "Juan, you have done a wonderful job of providing the research and procedures for the team. You ensure that all of the team members understand the systemwide rules for the work that they are doing. My intention now is to help you see the next area for your development as a manager.

"I've observed that sometimes you seem cool, aloof, and distanced from some of your team members. You are using facts, research data, and logic to communicate at times when the other team members are coming from a more creative, brainstorming, innovative, perhaps even emotional place. Sometimes you shut down their creative brainstorming with judgmental questions and comments. I suspect you are not aware that this is happening. I see times when you could do a better job of engaging and collaborating with your team members in a way that encourages them and invites creative, new ideas to be discussed. I'd like to explore with you the importance of communication styles and how they impact our conversations with team members. Are you open to doing this?"

When Juan has agreed, Kristi could offer to share a model for communication styles with him. Providing context is vital for understanding to occur. Any time people are being reprimanded, they will need more time to process the feedback and understand the context in which the feedback is relevant.

Another scenario occurs when you need to make it clear that the issue is serious. Say so. Say something like, "This issue is bigger than I suspect you understand. I want you to take this very seriously because if this is not resolved, it could cost you the trust of your team members (or your job)." Star performers sometimes make career-derailing mistakes. We may have been derailed without being aware that this has happened. This is when an excellent peer, manager, or leader whom we trust can serve as a mirror to help us see ourselves. We serve as a mirror by holding up our perspective on what has happened and providing time for reflection by asking questions that help the employees think through their actions and the next steps. Sometimes holding up a mirror is helping the people we are coaching to see themselves the way management sees them, especially when the issue is so serious that it could derail their career.

Getting Your Employees Where They Need to Go

If your employees have gotten off track, then it might take some work to get them back on the right path. First things first, though: do you recognize the kinds of traits that hold your employees back when you see them? Marshall Goldsmith wrote *What Got You Here Won't Get You There*, in which he listed "Twenty Habits That Hold People Back from the Top." He gave me permission to share them with you:

1. *Winning too much:* The need to win at all costs and in all situations—when it matters, when it doesn't, and when it's totally beside the point.
2. *Adding too much value:* The overwhelming desire to add our two cents to every conversation.
3. *Passing judgment:* The need to rate others and impose our standards on them.
4. *Making destructive comments:* The needless sarcasms and cutting remarks that we think make us sound sharp and witty.

5. *Starting with "No," "But," "However":* The overuse of these negative qualifiers, which secretly say to everyone, "I'm right. You're wrong."

6. *Telling the world how smart we are:* The need to show people we're smarter than they think we are.

7. *Speaking when angry:* Using emotional volatility as a management tool.

8. *Negativity, or "Let me explain why this won't work":* The need to share our negative thoughts even when we aren't asked.

9. *Withholding information:* The refusal to share information in order to maintain an advantage over others.

10. *Failing to give proper recognition:* The refusal to share information in order to maintain an advantage over others.

11. *Claiming credit that we don't deserve:* The most annoying way to overestimate our contribution to any success.

12. *Making excuses:* The need to reposition our annoying behavior as a permanent fixture so people excuse us for it.

13. *Clinging to the past:* The need to deflect blame away from ourselves and onto events and people from our past; a subset of blaming everyone else.

14. *Playing favorites:* Failing to see that we are treating someone unfairly.

15. *Refusing to express regret:* The inability to take responsibility for our actions, admit we're wrong, or recognize how our actions affect others.

16. *Not listening:* The most passive aggressive form of disrespect for colleagues.

17. *Failing to express gratitude:* The most basic form of bad manners.

18. *Punishing the messenger:* The misguided need to attack the innocent who are usually only trying to help us.

19. *Passing the buck:* The need to blame everyone but ourselves.

20. *An excessive need to be "me":* Exalting our faults as virtues simply because they're who we are.

Do any of these jump out at you as places your employees may need guidance to get back on track? If so, read *What Got You Here Won't Get You There*. Correcting these habits is the best way to gain support from our peers, team members, and bosses. Defending behavior that pushes people away is a useless waste of time!

Summary

World-class leaders are not afraid of conflict because they know how to get individuals and teams back on track when a derailment has occurred. When you understand why people do not do what you want them to do and you know which development action to take to deal with the situation, your own confidence and leadership abilities grow. Knowing the common derailers and the questions to ask to help employees gain a broad perspective and stop negative behaviors are keys to your being able to create meaningful conversations for getting back on track.

Conversations for Accountability

Whenever I would mention my desire to accomplish something, a mentor of mine would ask, "How will I know when it has been accomplished?" He was looking for me to share with him the measurable results, and he wanted to get a commitment that I would inform him of the action steps and the results. A typical conversation between us would have sounded like this:

Shawn: *Bill, I want to create a great sales training seminar. Doing so builds on the things you have been teaching me, and I see it as a logical next step.*

Bill: *Shawn, how will I know you are making progress?*

Shawn: *Hmm, good question, Bill. I will prepare the content for a one-day sales seminar and create the draft copy of the participants' workbook by next Friday. I will also send you a note sharing my top three insights along with the presentation slides. I will summarize them in our phone call next month, okay?*

Bill: *Sure, that sounds great. I look forward the next time we talk to hearing more about what you are learning from creating the seminar.*

This conversation format would be repeated many times with the content slightly different depending on what I was working on. When I reflected back on it, I realized I accomplished and learned so much from him because he created this conversation for accountability each time I indicated I wanted to accomplish something.

Accountability

Accountability often has a negative connotation. Being a micromanager and being involved with too much detail are often confused with being a manager who has clear accountability expectations. A positive view of being held accountable by somebody else is that this person cares enough about you and your work to ensure that the work is done efficiently and is producing outstanding results. The person you are accountable to is paying attention to what you are doing, and he or she is responding based on how you do. You receive positive acknowledgement when you do something well, and you receive suggestions or nudging when something could be done better.

I recently completed a Leadership Index for the senior management team of a Fortune 10 company that is a global household name. When the management team ranked the abilities, personal accountability was number 1 on the list that all leaders in the organization must demonstrate. This company realizes that if the leadership team is not accountable, no one else is likely to be.

Individual Accountability Rippling into Group Accountability

I asked a leader of an organization I do a great deal of work with to complete a 360-degree feedback survey. He grudgingly went through the process and listened to the feedback from his staff. At his next staff meeting, he gruffly said, "I got my feedback, and I did not like it."

There was silence in the room for a while before he continued, "I reflected on what you said, and I am willing to acknowledge you are right. I am going to focus on what you told me would help me to be more effective in leading our organization. I am going to be accountable to address the feedback you provided me. Each month at our first staff meeting, I will share with you what I have been learning and how I am using what I am learning in my work. Oh, and I will also randomly ask two of you to share the same thing. Each month I'll ask you, 'What have you been working on in your own professional development, and how are you using it to be more productive at work?' I will give you candor and honesty, and I expect the same thing back in return."

By being open, honest, and accountable himself and indicating that he was going to ask the team to be accountable also, this leader created a thriving learning culture that made it okay to talk about what needs to be learned and how application works best. Sometimes the solution for getting things done within a group of employees is team coaching. This leader understood team coaching, and he held all of his team accountable as a result of this practice. I think he is a great role model for his team!

Engage others in positive ways, build caring relationships that explore what matters to other people as it relates to creating a meaningful future, and then have ongoing check-in conversations about how the group is doing—this is the spirit of accountability conversations.

I start coaching meetings by asking, "Where would you like to begin today? What is most important given what you have on your plate currently?" I also know that after I listen to whatever is currently the most important thing for us to talk about, we will also revisit the list of accountabilities and goals to update how we are doing against them.

Demonstrating personal accountability is doing what you say you will do. This requires three other competencies to be developed also: self-management, planning and organizing, and communication skills.

Communicating the Importance of Project Lists

One of the best steps managers can make toward building and delivering on personal accountability is to ask their employees to write down everything they agree to do on a project list. A project list is not the step-by-step plan of how someone will accomplish the project; rather, it is the menu of what the person has agreed to do or is responsible for.

Ask your employees to review their project lists every day or at a minimum each week. Suggest that when they review their project lists, they ask themselves, "What is the next action required for each item?" This embodies self-management and planning and organizing. Guide and role model with your own expectations how you will keep others informed of your progress. Share with your employees that your expectation is that if they realize they will not be able to complete something as expected, then they will create a conversation with whoever was expecting results. By explaining what is happening and asking for what they need (this embodies communication skills), they will build trust and safety in relationships with other team members too. Ask your employees to role model these actions consistently to others to demonstrate a high level of personal accountability.

As a manager, you need to role model your expectations for your employees related to how to follow up. Do what you say you will do. This is the core of personal accountability. With my coaching clients, we get the ball rolling in the right direction of a behavior change by identifying the most important step that needs to be taken. Then they e-mail or call me every time that they agreed to do that action to indicate that they did do it. It typically takes about 30 days of this for the habit to be well established so that they no longer need to report in on their actions. You can do the same thing with your employees and the people you are coaching.

This would be a good time for you to review your own learning journal that you have been keeping while reading this book. When you reread your journal, what do you notice about your own ability to get things done and stay accountable to yourself and others? How can you use what you learned in this chapter immediately in your management, leadership, and coaching practice?

Summary

"How will I know when you have accomplished the desired result?" is a great question to be in the habit of asking people you are coaching. The question requires them to think through the next action steps and to share how they will keep you in the loop on their progress. Encouraging the use of a master projects list, which includes reviewing the list together regularly, is another way to support employees in their being accountable. Also, as a manager, you are role modeling personal accountability in the way you create this type of conversation.

Conversations for Performance Reviews

One of my early managers, Steve Merrill, set the standard for me by providing an excellent framework for our performance review conversations. When he hired me, he provided me with a written description of the key accountabilities for the work I was to do in my role—the kind of accountabilities we discussed in the previous chapter. The morning of the first day in my new role, he gave me a list, along with a schedule indicating that I would be meeting individually with each of the key stakeholders for my position. He asked me, in turn, to give each of them a copy of the key accountabilities for my role and to discuss the list with them. Steve wanted to ensure that each of the stakeholders in my new role understood what was expected of me and that we had discussed this together up front as I was beginning the job. Steve was setting me up for success from day 1.

Each month Steve and I had a conversation about how I felt I was doing against the accountabilities. With the list of my key accountabilities in hand, he would ask me questions like these:

- What progress has been made this month?
- Where can I be more helpful to you?

- Are there any barriers getting in the way that you want me to know about?

About six months later, he asked me to go talk with six of my key internal customers and ask them these questions:

- What is working?
- What is not working?
- What would you like more of or less of from me and my team?

Steve then asked me to write a summary of what I realized from this feedback and how I would use it to continue developing my performance in the role.

For the end-of-the-year formal performance review discussion, Steve asked me to evaluate my own performance, first in conversation and then in writing. Then three days later, he would discuss with me what he agreed with and where there were differences in our viewpoints. This showed me he really heard me and considered my input before he made his own decisions. He provided me with suggestions and ideas, but he left it up to me to consider which ones to take action on. This review process was an outstanding experience that kept me engaged in my work and enabled me to add value to the organization in ways that were meaningful for both of us. I'm not a person who saves things like this, but I still have his written performance reviews from 20 years ago because they were so meaningful to me.

For people who are responsible for performance reviews, and that is likely to be all supervisors and managers—anyone who has an employee reporting to him or her—it's important to create the kind of ongoing performance review conversations that lead up to the end-of-the-year summary document, as Steve did for me in the above example. Doing so builds trust and accountability, and it enables relationships with key stakeholders to develop momentum so that their feedback in the review process adds value.

A Performance Feedback Process That Works

Begin with a Job Benchmark before people start in the role or at the beginning of a new year that shows clearly what is expected from the role, including the key accountabilities, natural talents, communication styles, and motivators that align with success in the role. Provide all of this information to the employees in writing when they begin the role or at the beginning of a new performance cycle, showing them clearly what star performance means to you. Decide together how often you will update each other on issues and progress.

The goal is to create conversations about how performance is going weekly and summaries monthly so that the employee will stay inspired and focused.

Make it clear up front that the end-of-the-year performance review document is a written summary of 12 or more conversations that have occurred during the year. Nothing on the written document at the end of the year should be a surprise to the employee. This is an ongoing conversation that enables feedback to be part of the normal way of operating.

What Causes Performance Reviews to Go Well?

Taking responsibility and spending the right amount of time on issues are two of the factors that contribute to a positive interview experience.

Taking Responsibility

Prepare your team members to be able to describe their performance results even if you are not there at the end of the year to do so for or with them. Rick Harrity shared with me that in his 10 years of professional work experience, all with the same company, there were 3 years in which he did not have a performance review discussion. In all three cases, the reason was that his manager had been promoted or had left the company and did not leave behind notes on his performance for the new manager.

Poor planning on the part of a manager hurt this employee. The first time this happened, Rick's manager had left the company unexpectedly a month before Rick's annual performance review was due. Rick told me that it was very challenging because he knew he had performed well in projects and assignments that were a stretch for him, but his manager had not documented this in his file. Rick wanted to be acknowledged for his growth, but the new manager brought into the organization from the outside did not realize the significance of Rick's growth during the year.

From then on, Rick took responsibility by tracking for himself what his performance accomplishments were. His new manager encouraged him to think about his performance review as **his** responsibility to be able to have both sides of the conversation if needed—to show what the manager's viewpoint would be as well as what his own experience was. Now if his manager leaves the company unexpectedly, he is prepared to demonstrate to a new manager what he has been working on, how he has added value to the organization this year, and what he is working on developing in terms of his own capabilities and skills for the future. This is wise coaching from any manager to his or her employees, and it occurs when you follow the process for regular feedback that I've outlined in this chapter.

Spending the Right Amount of Time on Issues

Amy Mountain, director of communications at Elizabethtown College, told me, "When holding a performance review discussion with a star performer, spend a commensurate percentage of time on the priority topic—for example, if a problem issue represents only 10 percent of the person's performance, but the remaining performance is 90 percent wonderful, spend 10 percent of the conversation addressing the expectation for change due to the problem, and the remaining 90 percent of the conversation endorsing the positive attributes of the employee."

Amy also went on to say, "Especially during the preparation phase before a performance review, I begin by asking a new employee to spend some time describing what job or work he or she would do if money weren't an issue or if there were no 'barriers' (for example, no bills to pay or no family expectations to meet). Particularly for young workers who may be developing their idea of what they 'want to be when they grow up' or employees who may be nearing retirement, the descriptions of what their dream job is can help a manager to build in opportunities to include possible elements of the dream job in future assignments. This way, the employees get to find out if the dream job really plays to their passions. Additionally, it causes the employees to feel much more loyal to the supervisor when they see the supervisor adding some elements of the dream job to assignments and referring to it in the written performance review document."

We found in our research that performance reviews that were tied to the individuals' goals and aspirations for their future were more inspiring and engaging for employees than reviews that were focused solely on the tactical day-to-day measurements of the current job. Create review discussions that involve the employees' current and long-term goals, and provide space for talking about how what is being done today builds to the future.

What Causes Performance Reviews to Go Poorly?

Hopefully, you have not experienced any of these examples yourself. It is helpful for managers or those who coach mangers to avoid these performance review pitfalls.

You may be surprised or amused as you consider these true examples of performance reviews gone bad:

- Not having a clear picture of the role and its accountabilities, and thus having subjective, biased feedback from a manager after the work is completed.
- Not holding regular conversations about how things are going, thus creating surprise negative feedback.

- Not including feedback from peers and key internal and external customers. Managers cannot see every aspect of their employees' performance.
- Not having a two-way conversation between employees and the manager.
- When managers tell the employees to write the review, and the managers do not have anything to add to it.
- When managers say something like, "I am sorry. I would have rated you higher, but your peers (or Tom) told me that you don't do XYZ very well, so I can't give it to you."
- When managers say something like, "Since we do not have any money to give raises this year, I'm not taking the time to write a review. Instead, I just cut and pasted from last year's review so there is something on file in HR."

Situations like those are so demotivating. Avoid them at all costs.

Competencies as the Foundations for All Performance Reviews

Let's take a look at the real-life case study in the box "Performance Appraisals." This is from a company that created a highly productive performance review system in which core competencies are integrated into all performance appraisals and employees are measured against the same core competencies. Departments assign the competencies by the role or position and by the level of leadership experience. The box shows the organization's one-page brochure that it gives to every employee. It outlines the expectations and process for performance reviews.

Structuring the Performance Review Conversation

If you worked in the organization whose performance review system is described in the box "Performance Appraisals," can

Performance Appraisals

What Is Our Competency Model, and How Was It Developed?

A cross-functional team identified the abilities employees need to help make the organization successful. Our competency model is intended to be flexible and will be adjusted to meet future needs as they arise.

The most important abilities were divided into two groups: core and leadership:

- *Core abilities:* Every employee needs to be skilled in the same core competencies.
- *Leadership abilities:* There are three subsets of leadership abilities:
  - *Emerging professional competencies:* Emerging professionals are employees in the early stages of developing leadership skills. They are seeking to grow into supervisory and management positions.
  - *Experienced professional competencies:* Experienced professionals have developed some leadership skills, and they may have achieved some formal responsibility in their positions. They may have up to 10 employees reporting to them.
  - *Established professional competencies:* Established leaders have a wealth of executive knowledge and leadership experience, and they have responsibility for several business areas and more than 10 employees reporting to them.

The three categories of leaders are not meant to be concrete steps. Rather, these groups represent milestones on a continuum of development as employees become proficient in the various competencies. Each employee's career path will be different based on his or her interests and goals. As someone develops more professional

(continued)

skills, it may be important for him or her to develop some of the leadership competencies before he or she is assigned any formal level of responsibility.

What Are the Core and Leadership Abilities Included in Performance Reviews?

The eight core abilities that all employees will have in their performance review include business acumen, interpersonal communication, listening, teamwork, planning, problem solving, quality orientation, and continuous learning or self-development. These are the essential skills that every employee needs to have as the "price of admission" to work in this organization. These skills can be developed and demonstrated in many different ways depending on the employees' role.

Depending on individual employees' level of leadership in the organization, they may have the following competencies evaluated in their performance review.

The first of the three levels of leadership competencies includes the eight competencies identified for the emerging professional:
1. Conflict management
2. Decision making
3. Delegation
4. Innovation and creativity
5. Negotiating
6. Priority setting
7. Time management
8. Development of effective teams

These competencies enable emerging professionals to gain a more formal level of leadership and lay the foundation for becoming experienced and established professionals.

The second level includes five competencies for the experienced professional: influence, developing and coaching employees, managing diversity, people reading, and inspiring others. These capabilities are for those who have some formal authority in terms of responsibility for leadership in our organization.

The third level includes four competencies for the established professional: flexibility and dealing with ambiguity, strategic thinking, leading multiple teams, and managing vision and purpose. Individuals with proficiency in all four of these competencies have the potential for greater influence over decision making, and they are set on a course to higher levels of senior management.

How Will the Organization Use These Core and Leadership Competencies?

They will be used to give employees the development opportunities necessary to move the organization forward to meet its strategic goals. All coaching, training courses, and development assignments will tie into the organization's competency model, which is in alignment with the organization's strategic goals.

How Will the Competencies Relate to My Job?

During your performance review, your manager will have an open discussion of your strengths and areas of possible growth in relation to the competencies. At that point, the two of you will develop an Individual Development Plan. This plan will outline a variety of opportunities to master the competencies and learn new skills.

you imagine the way you would structure a conversation with the employees about their performance and development?

Gail is a new manager who wants to be a star performer. In her organization, each person is calibrated on these core competencies:

- Business acumen
- Project management
- Interpersonal communication
- Business results
- Personal accountability
- Team collaboration

Gail asked her manager, "What does star performance look like in each of these areas?"

Managers need to be able to describe what the ratings "needs developing," "fully performing," and "outstanding" look like. As a new manager, Gail needs to understand each of these ratings clearly, so that she can identify where her employees are and how to help them develop. Management is about helping employees to understand exactly what outstanding performance looks like so that they will be able to reach that target and hopefully exceed it. Field visits or team meetings that maximize the understanding of what stars look like enable clarity and growth. Gail told me one of her key learning points was this: "Keep the competency model in front of you regularly. Ask your leaders how you are doing against it and what else you need to be doing to develop to be at the star level in each competency. Then track your progress to demonstrate your results."

An Ineffective Management Practice

It is important to work together as a team, right? Together everyone achieves more. In the organization above, Gail told me, "People are calibrated against their team members and put into a bell curve for performance ratings. But we managers feel as if we are sending the wrong message. We are saying working together as a team is vital and yet we are forcing competition because only 10 percent can be rated outstanding performers."

I encouraged Gail to step up as a manager and advocate changing this performance practice. She can focus on building team collaboration as a company competency and highlight ways to acknowledge and reinforce collaboration. If you are in this situation in your organization, speak up and influence those who are responsible for the performance management systems to create a team performance rating if you want to encourage collaboration and do not want to force a bell curve.

Summary

The performance review process that you establish with your employees, team members, and people you are coaching can have a significant positive impact if you create ongoing conversations based on key accountabilities and then follow up consistently. This chapter gave you specific actions to take to ensure that you are creating meaningful performance discussions that guide employees to understand what star performance looks like up front. This information will enable them to deliver the desired results. Managers who think performance appraisals are once-per-year discussions are making a big mistake. They risk having the employees become disengaged about the meaning of the work they perform and how it relates to the business.

Conversations for Recognition

Evan was inspired to learn a complex new skill, and with great excitement, she signed up for a team coaching experience. Early in the coaching process, it was clear that her team members were much better at learning and performing the new skill than she was, but she was so excited about learning that she did not pay attention to the difference in their ability levels. Evan saw herself improving each week and felt great about it.

Six weeks into the learning experience, during one of the sessions, when Evan was feeling great about her performance, the coach said to her in front of the team, "I never thought you would get this far!" The coach probably meant this as a compliment; however, the way it was said in front of the group caused Evan to feel deflated, and she lost interest entirely in continuing to learn. She immediately stopped working with that coach.

I share this because it's important that we are all aware of how the other person interprets what we are saying. Confirm that the positive compliment landed that way by saying, "I'd like to compliment you on your progress!" instead of saying something like, "I never thought you would get this far."

As another example, the senior managers of a client organization I was working with asked me to help them design a new employee orientation. They wanted all new employees to come together for five consecutive weeks to learn about the culture of the new company they were working for and about the ways the various departments worked together. So we developed the new program.

We set this up so that Tom and Davina, managers from different parts of the company, would co-lead the orientation sessions. We saw the orientation program as also fulfilling a second purpose, which was to recognize and reward experienced employees by inviting them to come to these orientation meetings to showcase what their department was doing and how they contributed to the organization.

We also created a luncheon session as part of the orientation program. The luncheons would be for both experienced and new employees. We knew that inviting star employees to have lunch with the new employees would help the star employees realize that they were being held up as role models.

We created additional activities to enable all of the new employees to meet all of the other new employees as well as the heads of each key department during the five-week group experience. We also invited the hiring manager to the orientation so that he could meet one-on-one over lunch with the new employees. The hiring manager was guided to create a conversation specifically for recognition to tell the new employees how excited and honored he was to have them on the team and why he believed these new employees would add value to the organization. These conversations for recognition paved the way for the new employees' positive integration into the new culture.

The Importance of Affirmation

Did you know that it takes five positive interactions to dilute one negative interaction in a relationship if we want the relationship to continue to grow? Of course, this goes for a working relationship just as much as it does for a romantic one, or one between friends. Fewer than five positive interactions to one negative interaction will lead to disengagement, separate lives not connected to the same agenda, or the end of the relationship. What could you do to make positive deposits intentionally into the emotional bank accounts you have with the key people in your work life?

Pointing out what someone did well is affirming. As Charles Schwab said, "I have yet to find the person, however exalted his station, who did not do better work and put forth greater effort under a spirit of approval than under a spirit of criticism."

Or as a fortune cookie recently reminded me, "Not even a schoolteacher notices bad grammar in a compliment."

When you are in a place where your fear of failure outweighs your desire to succeed, you will feel stifled. As a developer of star performers, it's important to create a habit of affirming even the smallest moves in the right direction when you see employees taking steps to move out of fear and improve their performance. It's important to look for the signs that things are moving in the right direction and talk about them. Encouraging your employees' learning and continuous improvement requires allowing people to share their mistakes and turning them into positive experiences. As a manager, you can guide the way employees think about or hold their mistakes. You can say and role model that we all make mistakes, and it is our ability to learn from them and apply that learning going forward that are worth recognizing. Applaud your team members who admit to doing something wrong but then discover how to fix it.

Gratitude over Criticism

Regularly pointing out the things others are doing well is a useful habit in building a positive emotional wake. Employees are being mismanaged if they are criticized frequently with no acknowledgment of their strengths and abilities. It is your responsibility as the manager to understand behavior patterns, communication styles, motivators, and natural talents so that you are able to see clearly what your employees can do well.

Point out to your employees how they can use their natural styles and talents to add value in your department. Doing so demonstrates you've taken the time to get to know the individuals well enough to play to their strengths and capabilities. Even when you discover employees who are round pegs trying to fit into square holes—in other words, they are not a good fit for their roles—you will still be able to point out what their strengths are and where they could take the package of what they bring to work and apply it in other roles that would be a good fit for them. This is recognizing who they really are. You will be able to do this easily when you have mastered understanding behavior styles, workplace motivators, and natural talents.

When you think of your last boss, what feeling do you notice? We create an emotional wake in relationships as a result of the conversations we have or do not have. When we point out what people are doing well, how they are moving a project forward, or the way they are adding value to the team, we are building a positive emotional wake.

When we criticize or try to fix other people, we are creating a negative emotional wake in the relationship. To break this cycle, focus on feeling gratitude and thanking others for what they do bring to the team. Your own energy will determine if the employees will hear what you are saying as diminishing criticism or opportunities for powerful, positive development. Ask for what you want clearly, with a tone that demonstrates that you see who the employees really are. Convey your belief that the employees will be able to perform the task (if not, they may be in the wrong roles, and that is a different conversation). Confirm that the employees understand your request. If the employees do not understand what you want from them, you may have to demonstrate it yourself, recognizing their learning style and providing the needed information to them in that manner. When employees take initiative and begin doing something in a new way, acknowledge their efforts with a sincere and specific thank you.

Remember the last time you worked overtime or during the weekend on a special project? If no one thanked you, I bet your emotional bank account with your boss took a bit of a hit. On the other hand, if your boss sent flowers, acknowledged you in a team meeting, or handwrote a thank-you note, you probably felt appreciated.

Acknowledging what people have contributed and thanking them for it may open the door for them to let go of bitterness and move on. If you observe conflicts with particular employees, look to see if you can find a positive intention on their part or a worthwhile value underlying their actions. If so, you can thank them for this. That may be just enough of a shift to guide the conflict into a conversation for resolution. After people thank you, it is hard to argue with them!

A Gratitude Exercise

Feeling gratitude enables us to create a positive emotional wake with others (even during times of change or conflict). I encourage you to be emotionally aware enough that you are able to come from gratitude and well-being even when you are handling something difficult. Here is a way for you to practice this:

- Make a list of the key stakeholders to your role.
- Identify something you could acknowledge or thank people individually when they have contributed to you and/or the team.
- Write a handwritten note or an e-mail (perhaps send a copy to their boss if that's not you!) indicating specifically what you appreciated that they did.
- Notice how you feel after doing this. Joyful?

Long-term positive results: Now watch as these people repeat those same actions and behaviors again and again because they were acknowledged positively.

Acknowledging others for their contributions also reminds us of the importance of building long-term relationships. When we endorse the strengths and natural talents that others bring to the table, they are more likely to do the same for us as well.

Gratitude in Action

Abha Patel is a brilliant conceptual thinker and strategic planner. She is on the high-potential track as a managing director in her global company. Abha had been with her organization for 10 years when she asked for the opportunity to work with me as an executive coach. When we began working together, she identified her goals as wanting to be a more effective leader and increase her team's effectiveness. We completed the 360-degree perceptual interviews, and we found that every person on Abha's team as well as all of her peers realized that she was a brilliant thinker. They all talked about her accomplishments and how smart she was.

When I asked them what they would like more of from her, the same thing came up in every conversation:

* Be humble more often.
* Thank the team members because you could not succeed the way you have without the contributions of others.
* Acknowledge people when they make improvements.
* Don't focus so much on what is wrong. You have been pointing out what people need to fix, not what people are doing well. Turn this around.

When Abha received this feedback, we agreed that one of her goals would be to begin to acknowledge one person each day for the contributions he or she was making to the team or to her work. She bought a box of thank-you cards and began to write one each day. Often when my coaching clients are beginning to develop a new habit, I have them e-mail me each day to indicate that they completed the assignment. The first day Abha e-mailed me saying, "I wrote my thank-you note, but I feel silly doing it. I wrote to a former boss and told him how much I appreciated that he taught me how to think in a futuristic way.

I do not think it will make a difference." The second day she wrote, "Still feeing silly looking for something to thank someone about, but today I wrote to my assistant and thanked her for working late on a report for me last night."

Within two weeks Abha told me she had increased the number of thank-you notes she was writing to two or three each day because it was so enjoyable and she was seeing how much people appreciated her notes—they were hanging in people's offices! She also told me, "My former boss called personally to say how much he appreciated my note. He said it made him feel grateful to have had the opportunity to work with me. That shocked me because he is the chairman of the board of another company and now lives in Singapore. Hearing him on the phone and realizing my thank-you note to him had made a difference and reconnected us—this thank-you note writing is now a leadership habit for me!"

Phrases for Recognition

There's more than one way to make employees feel appreciated. Here are some phrases you can use to get you started:

- I've noticed you are making great strides in moving your project forward. Even though you are not there yet, I wanted to let you know that I see your progress. Keep up the good effort.
- You have been on the job for only a few weeks, but I wanted to take a moment to thank you for joining us. I've noticed you are adding value by . . .
- When I went into the client meeting yesterday, I realized that the document we gave them looked amazing. I asked who created it and was told that you did. Thank you so much for the extra-special talent you have for making our proposals look great.
- Your conversation with me lifted my spirits, and I wanted to take a moment to thank you for inspiring me.

133

- I appreciated that you went out of your way to help me with . . .
- Staying late in the office to complete the report for the XYZ project was going above and beyond.
- You are the winner of the Excellence Award today!

People want to do more for those who acknowledge their efforts. If there is a behavior you want to see more consistently in people, thank them when they do it for you.

Summary

Knowing that it takes five positive interactions to dilute one negative interaction in a relationship gives us clarity that if we want the relationship to thrive, we need to acknowledge and affirm others. If we want to create a positive emotional wake with our teams, we will intentionally focus on pointing out what people are doing well, and we will celebrate successes and small steps in the right direction. As a manager, coach, or leader of high-potential people, you will see them flourish as you look for ways to thank them for the contributions they are making to your organization and team. Whom could you recognize in a positive way today?

Conversations for Succession Planning

According to Dottie Brienza, the senior VP of global talent management at Hilton Worldwide, the war for talent is happening now, and it will be even more obvious as the economy improves. In China, India, and several other countries, Hilton will need large numbers of new employees next year. It can't develop people internally fast enough to meet the demand.

Succession planning is vital because your star performers may be encouraged to explore options in other companies. Do your star performers know that you want to keep them and you are committed to their development?

The Talent Pool

Successful competition in the marketplace is correlated to a company's ability to attract, retain, and develop talent. Whether filling open management positions, staffing new roles created by growth and restructuring, or preparing for executive succession, how ready are you to fill key positions in your organization with star performers? The most important measure of your organization's long-term health is the talent pool that is being developed for key roles.

Results from Ernst & Young's Global Talent Management Survey have shown that companies that integrate and align business strategies with talent management deliver higher shareholder value. Those with the best alignment have had significantly higher financial performance—an annual return on equity that was 20 percent higher over a five-year period—than those that have not (from Ernst & Young's "Sophisticated Talent Management Programs Drive Business Results," May 24, 2010).

Charlie Tharp, executive vice president, HR Policy Association, shared that each year the association surveys its members to determine the top concerns of chief human resources officers (CHROs). The top two concerns reported in the 2011 survey are these:

1. Executive development and succession
2. Talent management

Moreover, executive development and succession was most frequently mentioned as the top concern on the minds of CHROs over the past four annual surveys. Similarly, talent management has also been at the top of the list in recent surveys.

Forward-thinking organizations and leaders are mining their talent pools now to deepen the engagement of existing stars while causing a whole new group of high performers to grow from within. When an organization intentionally considers how people will be developed for future roles, the practice is referred to as *succession planning*. Every company, no matter what its size, needs a succession plan.

Chris Pollino, responsible for executive talent development at Genentech, focuses on professional coaching for director-level and above employees. While speaking at a conference, Pollino said, "100 percent of the employees who went through formal coaching are still in the organization—it is a great retention tool."

A 2010 study from Rice University found that when outsiders join the executive suite, those outsiders succeed at cost cutting. But once these opportunities are gone, the outsiders lose effectiveness because they lack in-depth knowledge of the organization's culture and how to get things done within the communication patterns of that culture. In-depth knowledge is required for driving strategic initiatives moving forward. By developing leaders from within, an organization does not have to experience this. However, I do acknowledge it is not always possible to develop leaders from within. When an organization does need to bring in a senior-level person from outside, the best way to proceed is to match that person to a high-potential colleague who will appreciate the mentoring in exchange for help with navigating the organization's established culture.

Identifying Top Positions to Fill

Succession planning focuses development on future roles. Planning for leadership replacement begins by identifying the top-priority management and leadership positions. These may be the positions that are most at risk for vacancies and those with a likelihood of someone's leaving, followed by future positions planned to anticipate the growth of the business. In succession planning, an organization systematically looks at the existing teams and players, and it identifies where there are gaps. Each key position is identified, and then two to three people who are potential fits for development into that role are identified.

"Where am I on the succession plan?" is a useful question for a high-potential star to ask senior management. If your employee asks such a question, that highlights her ambition and awareness. It is not the only question she should be asking, though. Once the conversation is started, that employee would be wise to also ask, "What number am I on the line-up for the next role?" You may find there are three to five people you have identified as potentials for the role your star performer has her eye on. You may or may not want to provide clarity with regard to whether the employee is number 1 on the list. Many organizations will not want to be this specific and are unwilling to make guarantees about succession paths until the time of a promotion. If this is the case in your organization, confirm for your star performers that they are in the succession plan, but that you are not able to share what the line-up for promotions is because it has not been determined yet.

As a manager, if you are coaching star performing midlevel managers who have been told they are numbers 3 to 5 on a bench to move up, or if you are in a very flat organization and it is clear there is no growth potential, it may be wise to suggest that your star performers look at opportunities to move into other organizations. As you probably know from being a manager of managers, the higher up you are and the longer you are in a culture, the harder it is to move to a new company. If it would be a conflict of interest for you to directly suggest that some high-performing employees would benefit from looking outside the company because there is no growth potential available to them now, you may instead want to suggest they find a mentor who is not in your company. The mentor would then possibly be able to help those employees to explore other options.

Hiring with an Eye toward Succession Planning

By creating a department that hires entry-level employees and then designing career path and developmental opportunities for those employees to learn about other parts of the organization, you can save your organization thousands of dollars and countless hours. We did just this for a large software company. We designed the organization so that the customer support department was the feeder pool for development, consulting services, IT, and several other key areas of the business. We hired stars into the customer support team and intentionally developed them for future roles. After 6 to 12 months in their roles as customer support representatives, the employees were able to select a team they wanted to be on—these teams were development,

IT, management, and consulting services. The teams aligned to their long-term developmental goals.

While on these teams, employees were able to focus some of their weekly team meeting time on learning more about that area. For example, the consulting services team was made up of those members of the customer support department who aspired to move into consulting services. When the consulting services department needed someone to travel on site to help a customer with a technical problem, we'd ask which of these team members wanted the opportunity. As another example, the development team would often have a guest speaker from the programming department or would perform a research project with the results being turned over to development. This created a vibrant learning organization that inspired employees to want to become star performers.

Cultivating star performers who are on your team to become the superior performers of your future means they will be ready to step up as positions open. This has many benefits for the organization, including promoting internal candidates who have been specifically developed for a position. It also offers the opportunity to promote others in a domino fashion. These employees get up to speed faster than candidates brought in from the outside. The time it takes to be highly effective in the role is abbreviated for the employee who is already acclimated to the company culture, strategic planning process, and budgeting systems. It also saves a great deal of time and money in recruiting costs.

What Happens When There Is No Succession Planning?

Do you recall Angela from the Introduction and Chapter 2? She had the respect of both her management and the large group of people who reported to her. Angela was confident she was being developed to take on the vice president role when it opened up in the near future—the person who was in the role had signaled that she was close to retiring. Angela was told several times by senior managers that she was a high-potential performer who was going places. With 5 years of experience as a senior director in her department—2 years more than any other—and 10 years of experience in the department delivering services, she was by far the most qualified person for the VP role. So why didn't she receive the role when it became available? There was no one ready to take her position!

The CEO explained to Angela that she needed to have people ready to take her role and that the new VP hired from the outside would be moved into a new position once Angela had her own role covered. Angela would be promoted only after someone was successfully performing her current accountabilities. This midlevel management crisis for the organization raised the awareness of the importance of succession planning for all roles, not just the senior leadership team. In her department, they began to meet twice a year to evaluate all the key positions to identify two to three people who could move into the roles, and customized development plans were created for each person identified. Angela told me she is now an evangelist: "Succession planning is for all roles, not just the C-level positions."

"People development is not linear. People often think of succession planning as a stand-alone activity. It is not. It needs to be integrated into the talent management framework that influences all people development decisions," according to Steve Hart, AVP human capital management, Philadelphia Federal Reserve Bank.

It is a fact: we now live in a world where the demand for leadership greatly exceeds the supply available. In another recent research study, CEOs were asked what concerns they had for their company's future. The number 1 response was the absence of leadership talent.

Being Clear about What You Want

Debra Gmelin, PhD, is the corporate director of the Leadership Institute at Humana, a Fortune 100 health-care company, focused on life-long well-being. She wondered why more women were not advancing in their careers, despite significant leadership development. Women represented 69 percent of Humana's overall population, but only a small number of women occupied senior roles. This is common in most Fortune 500 companies. Debra shared this interesting reality:

We asked an analyst to review the Humana succession management data to understand how women and men were describing their desire to move to an executive role. For each senior leader, the organization wants to be clear on who will replace that individual if he or she is promoted, retires, or leaves the company—this is the succession plan. In our case, we have approximately 300 leaders that we track on a yearly basis. Each year, these people have the opportunity to update their online profile prior to annual succession planning conversations that take place with the CEO and the executive team. In their profile they are asked to share their past experiences and accomplishments, update any professional courses they have taken since their last update, and share what their career aspiration are and their desired next roles.

What we discovered from the analysis was alarming.

Of the succession population, men were four times more likely to declare their desire to move to the executive suite. Only 16 percent of the women declared this intention. In the dedicated profile section, where candidates have the opportunity to write in their career aspirations, the study revealed that men are decidedly descriptive on their intentions, such as, "In the next two years, I want to become the vice president of national accounts, and in the next five years I want to be promoted to the executive team." Women, on the other hand, write something like, "I want to be in a role where I can utilize my talents to make a significant contribution to the organization." Or, "I want World Peace!"

In succession conversations with the executives, there are two key areas for discussion. First, what impact and contribution did the individuals make to the organization last year? And second, equally important, what do they want to do going forward? The executive team becomes frustrated when they cannot easily ascertain from the profile data what people want to do to grow in their career. In the executive conversations, it is black or white: do the individuals know what they are committed to or not?

As a follow-up, and being curious, we invited the women in the succession management system to a focus group, sharing with them the information the study revealed. What we learned from these women was very interesting. Women believed that if they were competent and produced superior results, they would be recognized, rewarded, and promoted.

That is a myth.

In a Fortune 500 company, you'll find that most people are highly competent. If they weren't competent and capable, they would not have gotten the job in the first place, nor been able to keep it. Certainly, there are degrees of competencies, but it takes more than producing great work to get recognized and rewarded. Fact: You must state your desires for your own career path.

If you are managing employees who are not clear on their goals, consider communicating something like this: "It's important to take the time to be clear about what you want to create for your own career. Nobody else can do this for you. Put a stake in the ground and clearly identify where you want to be. Now is the right time to identify what your own goals are."

The Nine-Box Model

Many of my clients use a Nine-Box Model for talent management and succession planning (see Figure 11.1). In the model, companies identify the numbers of the boxes differently; do not assume that the numbers listed here are the same as your own organization's model. For example, what some companies call Box 1 is what other companies call Box 9.

This type of model is used to identify where an employee is currently in his or her career from a succession planning standpoint and also indicates what developmental opportunities will be made available over the next year. [This model is believed to

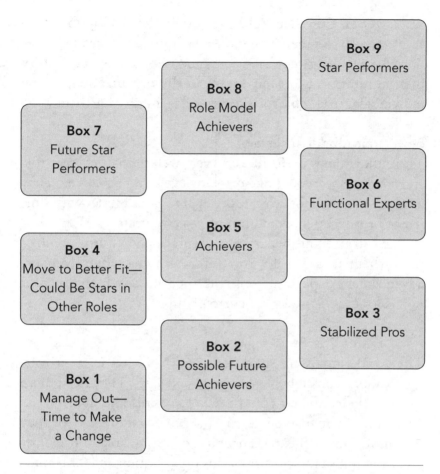

Figure 11.1 Nine-Box Model for Talent Management and Succession Planning

have originated as the "GE-McKinsey Nine-Box Matrix," *McKinsey Quarterly*, September 2008, following on the heels of the Boston Consulting Group's well-known growth share matrix.]

Box 9. Star Performers

These role models are performing above expectations, and they make significant impacts. They consistently demonstrate the potential to grow two levels above their current level during their career. They are ready for a significant increase in responsibilities, including cross-functional moves, within less than a year.

143

Next steps: Consider high-level visible stretch assignments to accelerate development and increase readiness for the next position. Acknowledge contributions, and reinforce the benefits of their committing to their career in the organization. These individuals are eligible for executive coaching immediately.

Box 8. Role Model Achievers

These individuals perform extremely well in their current role and could be promoted one or more levels in their career. They have the potential for cross-functional responsibilities with similar or broadened scope within one to two years.

Next steps: Consider developmental opportunities and/or place them in key roles to stretch and challenge. Manage advancement expectations. Invite them to coach and mentor others for the roles they are currently in.

Box 7. Future Star Performers

These individuals are solid performers in their current role, with room to possibly be promoted one level. They need more time in their current role to develop skills and appropriate behaviors. They may be new to the organization, and/or they may have had deep experience in the current area of responsibility but not in the culture of this organization and/or team.

Next steps: Provide ongoing feedback and coaching to increase current performance. Consider possible moves with a focus on increasing the breadth of their experience.

Box 6. Functional Experts

These individuals achieve results with a high level of organizational impact. They have been seasoned with deep expertise. They are satisfied to remain in their current role. They are valuable to the organization as long as their specialty remains relevant to the organization's needs.

Next steps: Encourage them to remain in their current position and area of expertise. Give them opportunities to mentor and coach others.

Box 5. Achievers

These individuals are performing well in their current role, and they demonstrate the desired behaviors for the culture. They may be new to the organization. They may be able to fill other roles within the same department or functional area.

Next steps: Provide ongoing feedback to increase performance in their current role and department. They are not currently being considered for promotional assignments.

Box 4. Move to Better Fit—Could Be Stars in Other Roles

These individuals have lots of potential, but they are in the wrong roles. They do not know how to do some important functions in their current roles.

Next steps: Explore other possibilities where their strengths, natural talents, and motivators would be a better fit. Encourage these employees to look at other possible internal positions, and set up interviews to facilitate a move within the next year.

Box 3. Stabilized Pros

These individuals are solid performers in their current role. They do not want to move, and they might not be meeting all expectations, but they fully understand how to do the important functions in their current role.

Next steps: Capitalize on the strengths these individuals bring to the team. Enable them to teach others the steps in performing well in the role.

Box 2. Possible Future Achievers

These individuals are new to the organization and role, and they do not yet meet the expectations of the role.

Next steps: Actively coach them for rapid performance improvement.

Box 1. Manage Out—Time to Make a Change

These individuals are not performing, and future improvements are not likely.

Next steps: Remove them from the organization as soon as a replacement has been identified.

What Are You?

If you were responsible for the succession plan in your organization, where would you put yourself?

Organizations use a Nine-Box Model to assist in both succession planning and performance management. The tool is intended to help managers frame their conversations with employees to set realistic expectations and identify next steps in developmental plans given current realities. Individuals who are identified as being in box 9, 8, or 6, for example, are given access to any types of developmental support they request. They often have business coaches and mentors because they are the star performers who are expected to be leaders today and tomorrow.

Summary

Succession planning is part of your job as a manager. Thinking about where your employees can grow and how they may be able to develop skills and experience that will serve them in preparing for future roles is vital to your success. The higher you go in an organization, the more likely it is that you will be included in succession planning for key roles. Begin to prepare yourself for these important conversations now by considering whom you could develop to be ready for your own role as well as what areas of the organization would benefit from having members of your organization grow into those roles.

Inspiring Excellence

Congratulations on being the kind of person who is committed to being a world-class manager and leader! You are someone who is focused on inspiring excellence in others. How do I know this about you? Because you invested the time, energy, and money to read this book.

What will it take for you to be successful and stay committed to sticking with this process of developing star performers? Getting your message across to the people you are developing requires layers of conversations to take them to new heights. Luckily, you are the kind of person who has the stick-to-it ability to make it happen.

Also, you will become an even more successful person yourself by applying these ideas.

Trust yourself, and have the patience to practice what you have learned here. Will you believe in yourself and your ability to get to the next level as a developer of star performers? If so, you will be a world-class manager, and you will serve the people you want to influence by mastering the conversations you have learned here. You will get dramatic results. You can develop successful people on your team and throughout your company. You now have clarity of focus on what to say to develop stars. I've coached executives and leaders from start-up entrepreneurial firms, top Fortune 500 companies, and world-class businesses, and I've developed award-winning, high-performing teams. I know these conversations work.

Push yourself, let yourself grow, and share what you are doing and learning. Step up yourself. Believe you can do this. Your own mindset will determine how far you can go with these tools. Don't be a person who does things halfway. Be on the journey to outstanding results for yourself and others. This is excellence.

Managers and leaders are responsible for clarifying success factors, co-developing learning objectives, enabling learning, addressing barriers, discussing and reinforcing progress, providing day-to-day performance-related feedback, and being accountable for the development planning of the team as a whole. Have the confidence to step up to new behaviors and new skills, and take your own life to a new level. You can have success uncommon in most people's lives if you apply what you have learned here. Are you willing?

When they get into a new endeavor, most people think, "I don't know how to do that," so they stop. The really successful people are the ones who say, "Hmm, I don't know how to do that, and I want to, so I am going to put it on my own to-do list to learn how." If you are thinking that you don't have the resources and tools to become a world-class leader, it's an excuse that does not serve you. I promise you that there are people who were much worse off than you are who are now molding star performers in the area they decided to focus on.

Full Engagement

Do you recall Victor from the Introduction?

After successfully holding three key positions in IT, market research, and operations in the midsized company, Victor, a star performer, was promoted to vice president of finance. He was thrilled by the promotion and excited to make a difference for the company. Victor was known for his analytical abilities—he could grasp the big picture and the details, easily seeing what would be needed in the future. One year into the new position, more than 60 percent of Victor's staff had resigned from the company, complaining in exit interviews that his leadership style was the reason they decided to go. Victor was shocked and was even more surprised when the vice president of human resources told him that he needed to dramatically change his leadership style if he was going to be able to keep his current job.

Victor had succeeded in every prior position; this was the first time he was stumped and not sure what to do to resolve the issue. This was also the first time he had a large team he was responsible for leading. Victor made an appointment with his CEO and requested some help. "My staff is leaving," he said. "They're saying my leadership style is the problem. I realize if I do not fix this, I will not be successful here. I want to resolve this, but I need help. I do not know how to turn this around." That is when the CEO called me, asking if I would develop a VP of finance who is a star performer in the analytical and technical aspects of finance but who needed help to be able to lead and engage his staff so they would want to do the work in his department. When I first met with Victor, his question was: "Will you show me how to fully engage staff members so they are motivated?"

After I've met with coaching clients to determine what they want to focus on in our conversations, I take two important steps. First, I have the coaching clients complete assessments that help us understand their natural talents, motivators, preferred communication styles, and emotional intelligence. These assessments give us the whole picture of who the clients really are. Second, I conduct perceptual interviews and/or 360-degree feedback surveys to reveal the perceptions that peers, bosses, and team members have of the people being coached. When I did this for Victor, it was very clear that he was a star performer in his ability to see the whole picture and to dive deeply into the details at the same time. Victor was highly motivated, in practical ways, to measure results and to solve complex problems and see the future. His lowest motivator was to support or develop people. This combination enabled him to add great value, but it was not a match to the role he was currently in. When we benchmarked his position—meaning that we had his boss and peers complete a 40-minute online assessment that gave us a clear understanding of what they expected from his role—it was clear that he was not a natural fit for their expectations.

Over the course of our coaching sessions, Victor acknowledged that he would rather be an individual contributor in a senior executive role engaged in strategic planning and analysis of future needs for the business than a manager involved in day-to-day interactions with the people on his team and elsewhere in the company. Now Victor had a decision to make: did he want to force himself to do something that was not fulfilling to him, or did he want to follow his own passions? Fortunately, Victor chose the latter, and our work evolved into helping him find and create in his current company the right opportunity that played to his natural talents and motivators.

I love serving people to help them identify their natural talents and put them to work in meaningful ways as star performers. Part of being a world-class manager and leader is developing the know-how and ability to spot when people will be a great fit for a particular role and future roles in the organization. Another part is being able to help employees who are not a good fit for a particular role to understand that and move on without bitterness or anger toward the organization. Your ability to understand communication styles, motivators, and natural talents enables you to see how best to develop your team members' talents for the future.

Perhaps you are wondering why Victor did not want to manage and lead people. He asked me the same question, and this is what I shared with him.

Google's Search for Good Managers

At this point, I suspect we both agree that managers play an important role in the learning and development of the people who report to them. Could you go so far as to say that the relationship with a manager is more critical than the strategic plan, HR initiatives and benefits, and the training offered by the company in improving employees' performance? That is what Google's internal study of good management revealed for their organization. In this self-study, Google identified what could be called "the eight habits of highly effective managers." In order of importance at Google:

1. Be a good coach.
2. Empower your team, and don't micromanage.
3. Express interest in team members' success and personal well-being.
4. Be productive and results oriented.
5. Be a good communicator, and listen to your team.
6. Help your employees with career development.
7. Have a clear vision and strategy for the team.
8. Have key technical skills so that you can help advise the team.

In an article in the *New York Times*, Adam Bryant pointed out that having technical skills, while important, is at the bottom of Google's list, which might be surprising given the technical nature of their business. According to Bryant:

> Technical expertise—the ability, say, to write computer code in your sleep—ranked dead last among Google's big eight. What employees valued most in their managers and leaders were even-keeled bosses who made time for one-on-one meetings, who helped people puzzle through problems by asking questions, not dictating answers, and who took an interest in employees' lives and careers. —Adam Bryant, "Google's Quest to Build a Better Boss," *New York Times*, March 12, 2011.

Managers are successful in Google because they care about developing world-class star performers! They help and support team members in their learning and development. The relationship between the managers and leaders and their team members is the critical factor in employees' learning and performance improvement. Do you want to support and help people grow based on their goals? Are you passionate and on fire about doing this on a day-to-day basis, thereby inspiring excellence?

It is okay for Victor to focus on his passions and to acknowledge that being a superstar manager of people is not what motivates him! Victor has a rare combination of abilities, including being able to see future trends clearly. If being a manager is not for him, it is best for him to accept this and focus on what really engages him so he can be a star performer.

Actions That Distinguish Great Managers

Work done by Marcus Buckingham and Curt Coffman, authors of *First, Break All the Rules*, focused on what the world's greatest managers do differently from other managers. The questions they asked employees to determine good management included these:

- Do I know what is expected of me at work?
- Do I have the materials and equipment I need to do my work right?
- At work, do I have the opportunity to do what I do best?
- In the last seven days, have I received recognition or praise for good work?
- Does my supervisor or someone at work seem to care about me as a person?
- Is there someone at work who encourages my development?
- At work, do my opinions seem to count?
- Do the mission and purpose of my company make me feel like my work is important?
- Are my coworkers committed to doing quality work?

- Do I have a best friend at work?
- In the last six months, have I talked with someone about my progress?
- At work, have I had opportunities to learn and grow?

Now I ask you, how would the people you are responsible for developing answer these questions? Would they say you inspire them?

In this book you've learned about the conversations a good manager, leader, and or coach engages in. Are you passionate about creating conversations for developing star performers?

Stating your intention about which type of conversation you want to create will enable you to move in the right direction with each individual and team you are responsible for developing. Encourage your team members to step back and reflect. Build in time for reflection during your team meetings. Share what you are learning and how you are developing your own capabilities.

Ask your employees, "How do you measure success?" Then share how you will measure their success. After that, all that's left for you to do is follow through and walk your talk. By doing this, you will create a learning organization.

Then imagine what happens when the CEO stops by randomly and asks, "What are you learning? How are you using what you are learning?" You will be able to share something worthwhile and confidently ask the CEO to share his or her recent learning too—the conversation will be memorable!

As a manager and coach, you know that the people you are working with will have questions about the ideas you share with them and about how best to apply what they are learning. I would love to hear your specific questions and comments, and I invite you to visit me at www.ShawnKentHayashi.com to ask your questions and review other people's questions too. In the meantime, here are some questions I've recently been asked that I thought you might appreciate considering.

Question and Answer Session

All of these questions were asked of me in coaching sessions with star performers.

James: *How do you handle it when one of your employees also has an intimate relationship with your boss? For example, my employee Margie is my boss's daughter, and she's leaving the office around 2:30 three days each week to watch her son play baseball. She does not come back to the office afterward, and it is clear that she is not working the required 40 hours each week. Now other team members are complaining that she is getting special treatment. It is clear that my boss knows this is happening, and he has done nothing to correct the situation with his daughter.*
Shawn: *First, consider how you would handle this if Margie were not related in some way to your boss. What would you do?*
James: *I would mention to her that while she does not have set hours, she is expected to be at work for a minimum of 40 hours each week. I'd tell her she needs to make it obvious to the team how she is making up the time that she is taking off to watch her son play baseball.*
Shawn: *Great; I agree with you, James. Would you be willing to share with your boss the conflict this is causing on your team and share what you want to say to Margie? If you say you want to make him aware of the situation before you talk with Margie in the event that he feels the need to influence this communication first, then he will be supportive of you if she comes to him later complaining about your actions.*
James: *Yes! I can do that. And boy is it frustrating having someone on the team who is related to my boss.*

★ ★ ★

Tom: *I'd like to have several managers in my organization begin to coach others, but I'm not sure how to measure the effectiveness of doing this. What do you use to measure the results of your coaching? (Or another version of this that I hear is, "My executive manager just said to me, 'Show me the measures that demonstrate what you have accomplished. Justify the time you spend developing others and why it adds value to the*
organization.' What do I do now?")

Shawn: *There are six measures that can be tracked during a coaching relationship. This system works best when the people being coached take responsibility for creating a learning journal and integrating these measures into the content they are using as part of their journal:*

1. Activity: *How often are you meeting?*
2. Reaction: *What do you feel about the experience?*
3. Learning: *What was the content of the learning?*
4. Application: *How did you use what you learned?*
5. Business impact: *What impact did the application have on your business?*
6. Return on investment (ROI): *How did that impact dollars in your organization?*

Ask the people who are being coached to track this as they engage in the coaching relationship. Indicate that they will be expected to write a summary of their learning. The coachees may be asked to provide it to their sponsor if the organization is paying for the coaching relationship.

★ ★ ★

Rita: *You mentioned "Job Matching" and "Job Benchmark." What do those terms mean?*
Shawn: *A Job Benchmark is a Talent Audit on a specific role. A Job Benchmark can be constructed when the key stakeholders to a position identify the key accountabilities performed in a role and use our online Job Assessment to understand the attributes that are vital for success in the role. Job Matching can be accomplished when candidates complete the Talent Audit and we are able to see how closely they match the Job Benchmark. I use these tools in my work with organizations.*
Rita: *What can we do when the current employees' skills and abilities do not match the work that needs to be done? In other words, there is not a match between the Job Benchmarks and the people currently in the roles.*
Shawn: *Coach the current employees to understand where the gap is. Help them to come to clarity and understanding about how this role does*

not play to their strengths. Point out roles, departments, or organizations that would be a better fit for them. When people have experienced the Talent@Work seminars, those for whom such gaps exist between their jobs and their abilities have seen these gaps for themselves. The seminars have enabled people to become aware of the types of roles that would be better matches for their abilities.

★ ★ ★

Paulette: *How do you handle the challenge of supervising or mentoring people who are in the job you used to have, or conversely, the challenge of working for a boss who used to have your job? Twice I've been in jobs that were available because the previous people in those jobs were promoted, and I have found that it can be difficult for those people to "let go" of the previous position. They know how they did the job, and they often want it done the same way.*

Shawn: *Create Job Benchmarks so you understand what the current expectations of the roles really are. When you know you are a great match to the Job Benchmark, this knowledge will help you overcome the issues posed by a boss or mentor who had the role. You can look at your own Gap Report that shows the difference between the Job Benchmark and your current abilities.*

★ ★ ★

Andy: *How do I develop a high-performing team from scratch?*

Shawn: *Designing high-performing teams begins with the Job Matching Process. There are four steps involved with the Job Matching Process:*

Step 1. Identify the specific needs of the work to be done in the position:
- *What are the key accountabilities of the role?*
- *What work has to be done well for success?*
- *Which communication style is needed given the key accountabilities this role is responsible for?*

○ *Which workplace motivators are rewarded by the work being done?*

○ *Which natural talents need to exist and then be fully mastered for success in the role?*

To make answering these questions easy for you, I have an online assessment that enables you to evaluate a job as the first step in the Job Matching Process. Check out www.TheProfessionalDevelopment Group.com for more details.

Step 2. *Identify the characteristics in the following areas that the person needs to have:*
○ *Preferred communication style*
○ *Workplace motivators*
○ *Natural talents*
○ *Emotional intelligence*

To make identifying these characteristics easy for you, I have an online assessment that enables you to evaluate these areas in your own customized Talent Report. Check out www.TheProfessionalDevelopmentGroup .com for more details.

Step 3. *Compare the needs of the position to the individuals in the role. To make this easy for you, we have an online assessment tool that will generate a Gap Report that will show you 55 dimensions of comparison. The report will indicate where there is alignment as well as where there is a need to pursue development or to delegate that part of the role to someone else.*

Step 4. *Create an individual coaching plan for the individuals in each role to support their success in achieving the goals for the role. Yes, you probably guessed this, my company is able to do this as well. Using the results from the Job Benchmark and from your own assessment, we can provide you with a customized Individual Development Plan (IDP).*

★ ★ ★

Andy: *You've described how to develop star performers and high-per-forming teams, but what about when people are not star performers?*
Shawn: *It is not a requirement that everyone on your team be a star or high-potential performer who is promotable by two levels. You may want a few people on your team who will be Steady Progressors, who will want to stay in the role for many years. Star performers are often eager to move, to be promoted, or to have your position. Unless your function is a feeder pool for the rest of your organization, you'll want to balance the number of star performers you have with the needs of your business. Someone who is not a good fit for the work being done needs to be coached through a conversation for getting back on track.*

★ ★ ★

Tamara: *I am the coach to a VP-level star performer who is reporting to the CEO of a publicly traded company. This CEO is possibly abusing company resources by having two of the employees focus most of their time on his personal projects that are not at all related to the business. These two employees have asked their boss, a vice president, if this is legal. One of them saw a recent news report about someone in another company who went to jail for making it look like he was doing one thing when in fact he was doing something else—exactly the type of things the vice president's CEO is doing. The VP is feeling uncomfortable observing what is possibly unethical behavior, and she is not certain how to approach the situation, since it is clear her boss, the CEO, does not seem to be concerned about the ethics of the behavior he is engaging in. If you were the vice president's coach, how would you advise her?*
Shawn: *This advice would be the same no matter what type of unethical behavior was being observed. I would ask the VP if she would be willing to discuss this issue with corporate counsel by saying something like this: "I would like to check in with you to share something that is going on with my team and our CEO. I am not sure myself where the lines are, and so I wanted to seek your opinion on this, since it relates to our CEO (provide details here). Perhaps it would be worth it to get an outside opinion?"*

If there is not a corporate lawyer on staff that the VP has access to, she could find an outside lawyer who specializes in the VP's industry. The VP could then ask that lawyer what is over the line and how can she can protect her organization for the future.

Once the legal situation was clear, the VP could then arrange a conversation with the CEO and share what she has learned by saying something like this: "I want to protect us all from something that may not have been clearly understood. I myself did not know where the line was on XYZ, so I spoke with (corporate lawyer), and I learned that it is not advisable to have company employees doing XYZ. I will be asking them to change their focus tomorrow unless you have another way you would prefer to handle this?"

★ ★ ★

Amit: *My boss is neglecting to develop the star performers on our team. He is focusing on developing only the underperformers because he says that they are the weak links and he does not know how to identify who the star performers really are. What can I do? I am a star performer, and I want to be developed in our company's high-potential program.*
Shawn: *Talk with your boss, and highlight that a good indicator of a high-potential star is having approximately 20 personal skills above the mean as well as an above average clarity score in Acumen on the assessments I mentioned earlier. Star performers produce 12 times more than average employees. This* Human Capital Magazine *article, "End 'Equal Treatment' Today! Focus on Top Performers" (HC Online), will provide more information that will help you in speaking with your boss about the importance of identifying star performers: www.human resourcesmagazine.com.au/articles/0f/0c020e0f.asp.*

Explain to your boss that by benchmarking jobs and ensuring that the individuals are properly aligned to the jobs, he will be able to focus on developing more stars and helping the poor performers to move into other roles that are better suited to their strengths. If after two to three conversations on this topic he still does not listen to you on this subject, then it is likely time for you to find another boss who is interested in making a difference by developing star performers.

159

★ ★ ★

John: *What is one of the biggest mistakes you've seen managers make when thinking they were inspiring star performance?*
Shawn: *Filipe gave Barbara a "special project assignment." She was excited to be selected for this high-visibility project. Filipe also gave Lindsey the exact same "special project assignment." But he did not tell either of them he had given the other individual the same project. The employees began to work on their project, which required that they research and talk with others. Over time it became clear to them that they had been given the same special project. They did not understand why Filipe would have done this. Can you think of any reasons why managers would give the exact same assignment to two employees and not tell them about the other team member's doing the same thing?*

Here are some of the answers I've heard when I have asked managers the question above:

- *Filipe forgot that he had given the assignment to one of them.*
- *Filipe was comparing their results to determine which one to promote.*
- *He was watching to see how they would handle the inevitable conflict that would arise as they realized someone else was stepping on their toes and taking action on their special assignment.*
- *He was planning to keep only one of the two employees because he had to downsize his department. He needed to determine which one should go.*
- *He wanted to see if they would work together as a team once they realized he had given them both the same assignment.*
- *Filipe was trying to decide which one to develop for his own role, and he had to see how they would handle conflict and politics in order to decide which one would be best.*

Do any of these options make sense to you? Would you ever use this strategy to accomplish one of the goals on this list? Could this somehow be a way to drive employee excellence?

This is a useful discussion in management training because it helps managers to hear different points of view about how we engage with our employees for the sake of inspiring employee excellence. Some people feel very strongly that this is not a wise way to build team spirit, and I agree. I have seen this strategy used in two different organizations, once by a CEO and once by a director, and in both cases, they expected that the best person would rise up and possibly even collaborate with the peer. They expected to be able to evaluate the two for future leadership possibilities. They expected that either Barbara or Lindsey would say, "Checking in about this assignment, I have realized that someone else is doing the same thing. How do you want me to handle this?" In both cases, the managers' strategy backfired and created a division on the team and ill will. Barbara and Lindsey did not want to work together in the future, and both lost trust and faith in Filipe as a leader.

Sometimes managers do something with the hope that it will produce great results, and then it backfires. How can managers get the right kind of feedback when they are making mistakes that will frustrate team members? How can they find out when they are not inspiring employee excellence?

Managers need to observe their employees' body language and have regular check-in conversations asking, "How are you doing?" to create the openness in which employees will feel comfortable to discuss when their manager is off track.

Summary

You are inspiring because of your commitment to your own learning. We've come a long way together. Thank you for your commitment to being a world-class, star performing manager, leader, and coach. I look forward to hearing from you as you apply these ideas to your own management practices. Your insights and questions would be gifts to me. If you are willing to reach out to share what you have found most useful in this book, please do so! E-mail info@TheProfessionalDevelopmentGroup .com. Thank you.

Creating Star Performers with a Focus on 24 Vital Skills for Success

Here we'll focus on 24 abilities that I use frequently as part of individual coaching work with clients. We measure acumen, motivators, behavior preferences, communication style, and competencies. Here we're focusing only on skills; however, in coaching someone, it is very useful to look at all dimensions of the person before beginning to dive into one area.

Some abilities have more steps or depth required to teach them; you will notice I've written more about some of the skills than I have others.

As a coach or manager, when talking with someone you are developing, you'll need to adapt the information below to your organization and industry. These examples are intended to be useful to you as triggers for what you can share to inspire new thinking and action steps for development. Sharing your own story about how you developed a particular ability, as well as the changes you made in your thinking and behavior, will be very useful to the person you are coaching. Consider this a framework that you can fill in or use to help you develop your own conversations peppered with your own examples.

Conceptual Thinking

What is the concept you want to convey? Can you see the big picture and the details? Be clear about where you are starting and your current reality.

Expand your view, and allow in all the relevant information—look outside at the important, most relevant factors in the environment.

People have a tendency to look too narrowly at their current reality or to focus too broadly, trying to look at every single point of data that relates to the issue. When you look too narrowly, you will not see the big picture and your conceptual thinking will be fuzzy. For example, if Emily wants to be moved into another role, but she is focused on why her current boss does not like her, she will miss the big picture showing that other managers in the organization do value her contributions and that there is a pathway into a new role. Because she is stuck in the story that her boss does not like her, that thinking is limiting her ability to grow. Emily is not using conceptual thinking skills—she is thinking too narrowly.

When you do not filter and you look too broadly, it is easy to become overwhelmed by too much data. Conceptual thinking is creating a framework that is focused on the big picture without creating information overload or diving too deeply into details. So how do you do this? By compiling insight in a meaningful, useful way.

In *Being Strategic*, Erika Andersen outlines three steps, which I will explain below:

- Become a fair witness
- Pull back the camera
- Sort for impact

I use these steps and my own examples to explain how people can become clear on what conceptual thinking is, to create their own framework, and begin to practice.

The idea of becoming a "fair witness" comes from Robert Heinlein, who invented a fictional profession in which people are trained to be absolutely impartial in their assessments and to speak only from their direct observation, without inference or speculation. If you point out a red barn and ask a fair witness what color the barn is, he will say, "It appears to be red on this side." Are you stating things as they really are? If so, that is being a fair witness. Are you ignoring facts that aren't convenient, or are you assuming some things are not important because you do not want to factor them into your thinking? That is being an unfair witness. Include in your thinking the full picture of "what is." Ask yourself, "What am I missing, and what am I misrepresenting by not including it?"

Your "pulling back the camera" is similar to a camera's panning back, enabling the photographer to see the larger view. Perhaps in a movie you see a flower, and then you see flowers in a garden. Then the scene pulls back, and now you see that the flower garden is in a churchyard. Then the camera pulls back again, and you no longer see the details of the flowers in the garden, but you see that the church is in a small English country village. Each time the camera pulls back, there is more clarity about the context.

You can do this in your thinking as you look at a goal, a problem, or an issue. If you are responsible for marketing in a global business, you may be asking yourself how you can gain more market share. New data has shown that your core product is not selling as well in the United Kingdom this year as it did in years past. The dramatic drop had you thinking initially that you needed to do a deep marketing campaign in the United Kingdom. You wonder why the U.K. market has dropped so dramatically. As you pull back the camera in your own thinking and look at the larger situation around this issue, you look at all the markets. Now you see that the product is performing very well in Asia, where the sales numbers have increased amazingly—by the amount of the decrease in the United Kingdom. All the other markets have stayed the same. You wonder why. You pull your thinking camera back a bit more. You look at the client lists from the two marketplaces, and you realize that your top customer in the United Kingdom has moved its ordering facilities to Asia. The broader view that pulling back the camera has given you has enabled you to see the big picture of what is really happening. You might not need to create a new marketing campaign for the United Kingdom.

Change and enlarge your perspective by asking yourself, "How can I get a broader picture? What would I look at if I pulled the camera back?"

Sorting for impact is distinguishing the facts and events that are most relevant from those that are not. If you want to cost-effectively remodel your office building or home, you find out which walls are load bearing walls first, before you begin designing the new floor plan. The load bearing walls are relevant to keeping the integrity of the structure. Similarly, when considering an issue, ask yourself which are the load bearing components and which are not. If your new employee shares that he is anxious about going on site at a customer location to deliver a presentation to the company's president, you want to distinguish the facts. Is the issue that the employee is uncomfortable with the content and does not feel he has learned it well enough yet? Or is the real issue that there is a problem with this customer and the employee thinks he is walking into a problem account with challenges that are over his head? Or is there another issue that is more relevant to creating a solution?

Think about an issue or challenge you want to work through. Now take these steps:

- Develop a compelling question, idea, or concept that you have had an interest in exploring.
- Looking through blogs or websites or simply observing people, processes, or situations can trigger some topics you would like to consider in expanding your conceptual thinking.
- Ask yourself, "What ideas am I most interested in thinking about and understanding more deeply?"

Conflict Management

Our ability to identify differences in opinions and beliefs is the first part of conflict management. Some people, like Bob, are tuned out to differences. As soon as two people express a different way or path to accomplishing something, Bob unconsciously leaves the room. He does not have confidence in his own ability to facilitate a conversation that comes to resolution in a win-win way, so instead, he goes into passive avoidance mode and sweeps issues under the carpet. Bob has lost the respect of his employees as a result of this pattern of behavior. He does not have well-developed conflict management skills.

As a result, innovation and creative thinking were squashed on Bob's team, and he did not understand why. When people are afraid of conflict or differing ideas and they do not know how to facilitate differences of opinions, interpretations of current reality, intuitions, and feelings, then team collaboration, creativity, and innovation do not occur. For Bob to develop conflict management skills, he first had to be willing to see and hear when differences were being expressed.

In my previous book *Conversations for Change,* there is a chapter on creating conversations for conflict resolution. In it I shared that there are several types of conflict:

- Me against myself (a me-me conflict)
- Me against another (a me-you conflict)
- Me caught in the middle between two people or teams against each other (a me-them conflict)
- Me against others across several department or teams (me–big group conflict)

If we do not acknowledge the conflict, we will go numb, lose clarity, shut down, give in, comply, acquiesce, or abdicate our own needs. We may not even be aware that we have done this. So the first step in building conflict management skills is to raise our own awareness about when these things are happening. If this is the case for you, begin by noticing when there are differences expressed directly or indirectly. Notice that it likely triggers you to feel fear. Let yourself feel the fear instead of being hijacked by the fear into an avoidance mode.

Moving through the Conflict

To move through conflict, begin by doing the following:

- Listening to the others' points of view without agreeing or disagreeing.
- Managing your own thinking when this kind of thought comes up: "I do not know how to handle this, and I don't want them to fight with each other. It is best not to discuss this any further." Instead, say to yourself, "I am able to facilitate resolution, and I am going to stick with this until I understand the issue well enough to be clear in myself what I think the next right actions are so we can move forward (instead of get stuck.)"
- Saying, "I'd like to sleep on this, and I will respond in the next day to what I am hearing."
- Letting your thinking evolve over a few hours or days to see what ideas bubble up for you and writing them down so you can watch your thinking evolve.
- Circling back when you said you would and then sharing your own thinking or responses to the differences.
- Giving direction and guidance if you are the leader of a team that is stuck.

What to Ask For

Depending on the situation, one of these questions will help you move forward. Pick the one that works best for you:

- I'm conflicted about an issue, and I would like to talk it out with someone who is unbiased and who will ask me questions to get me thinking in new ways. Will you do that with me?

- Is there something we are tiptoeing around that we would both benefit from discussing? When would be a good time for us to discuss this together, sharing our pros, cons, and various puzzle pieces?
- What would need to exist for us to work through this issue?
- What is it that I (or we) really want, and how can I focus on that?

Working Through Your Own Feelings

Amy Mountain, director of communications, Elizabethtown College, shares this anecdote about conflict management:

Recently, I had an employee in my department who suffered from almost crippling self-doubt when confronted with conflict even though she was incredibly motivated and she was a self-starter otherwise. At her request, I worked with her over a period of a year to help her develop resiliency when faced with conflict. It was a very challenging process, as it required me to be brutally honest with her when she was demonstrating negative behaviors. She was not aware of what she was doing that was creating more problems for herself. One of the things that we did was agree to a "code word" so that if she was falling into a behavior "danger area" while under stress or when confronting someone, I could say the code word within a sentence, and it would alert her that she needed to step back immediately from the situation, so that she could calm herself and not create any further damage. She escalated conflict without realizing she was doing so, and the code word helped her to back off. This tactic required deep trust and honesty between us, but it really worked, and over time it became a point of humor . . . in that we could look back and name a specific event a "code word moment." It ended up being a very interesting and rewarding professional development opportunity for both of us.

It's important to learn to work through your own feelings of anger before taking action. Be as knowledgeable as possible about what triggers you and the other person. This will enable you to maintain a calm demeanor so that you can move toward taking effective action rather than simply reacting to the other person's anger. Be empathetic, but don't become enmeshed in the other person's emotion.

Knowing Your Own Limits and Boundaries

Be clear about what actions you are able and willing to take, and comfortable in taking, and communicate those to the other people or team in an honest, calm manner. If you were the sales manager dealing with a conflict with another department about something that had fallen through the cracks, while speaking to both groups, you could say, "Providing great customer service is a commitment we all make in our organization, and when we do not do so, it crosses a boundary. As an organization, we did not live up to our commitment to our customers. Let's think about how we can fix this current situation for the client and then go forward in determining how to avoid making the same mistake. What ideas do you all have about how we could work together toward fixing this situation?"

Developing Your People-Reading Skills

Be observant of body language, eye contact, pace, voice, and tone in yourself and others. The following four communication styles are triggered into anger and conflict by the following:

- *Dominant Style communicators* experience conflict and anger when they feel they are being taken advantage of or when they feel the other people are not competent or focused on achieving results. Dominant Style communicators are not afraid of conflict, and they will immediately be direct and to the point with the issue.
- *Influential Style communicators* experience conflict and anger when they feel the other people are being too tight-lipped, cold, or aloof or they are droning on and on with too much detail. Influential Style communicators experience conflict if

they feel the other people are putting them down in a know-it-all, arrogant matter. They may complain as a way to be noticed and want help in dealing with the "offensive people" who hold views different from theirs. Influential Style communicators are highly verbal people who will need to share what they are thinking and feeling. In fact, they may gush about whatever is in their heart—not listening to them squashes their energy and causes conflict.

- *Steady Style communicators* experience conflict and anger when they feel they are being rushed, pushed, or forced to make a decision before they are ready to do so. They may not show their anger directly. It will likely come out passively. They will silently fume about an issue and may make sarcastic, snide comments to passively let off steam rather than directly addressing the conflict.
- *Compliant-to-Standards Style communicators* experience conflict and anger when they are urged to express their feelings or to be emotional or when the data presented is not accurate and there is not enough detail for them to make their own decision. They will likely need time to go away and think about this before they can respond directly. They will come back with the facts to support the "right answer."

Be aware of how you may be triggering conflict and anger in others, and respect the needs of each style just as you want others to be respectful of yours. Remain positive, direct, and nonjudgmental as you ask for what you need or want going forward.

Another resource for ideas in conflict management is *Perfect Phrases for Dealing with Difficult People* by Susan Benjamin.

Continuous Learning

You and your employees will constantly be learning new things. What do you think they might want to learn next? How do you think they prefer to learn?

- Read books, articles, or e-books that relate to your current and future goals
- Listen to CDs, webinars, or teleseminars
- Watch DVDs
- Participate in workshops, seminars, classes, or conferences
- Have a coach guide them

Stress the importance of people using their preferred learning styles. If you do not know your own preferred learning styles, over the next five weeks try each one and see what appeals to you. Which ones inspire you to take action and make changes? Most of my coaching clients like one or two modes of learning and say they don't learn as well in other modes. One of my recent clients who is a verbal processor, a CEO, told me he does not have time or like to read. He wants me to read the books for him and then share with him what the key concepts and actions are. That works best for him as we discuss how he can apply the ideas in the latest business books. When I come back two weeks later, he tells me in great detail how he applied the framework I shared to his own business. Then I share the next step in the learning and the key concepts from the next part of the book. He is a life-long learner who understands how he prefers to absorb new ideas.

Create a system to keep you focused on what you want to learn. By reading for 30 minutes each day, taking a class in a new subject, or keeping a learning journal daily about what new insights and Aha moments you have had, you will direct your focus on learning. This structure is what helps you continually enhance your capabilities and consistent learning. Do it until it becomes a habit that you do not have to think about. Then move on to the next skill or system you want to learn! This is the path to mastery in many abilities, and it is vital for success in our changing world.

Career-related courses and certifications may help you build your expertise in your field. This approach keeps you aware of and helps prepare you for change that happens in your workplace and industry, and it may even prepare you to move on to the next level faster due to your broader perspective.

When you have the belief that you can learn anything you need to know, you remove the glass ceiling of limiting beliefs. If someone else has been able to learn how to do something, then so can you. If you want to, if you are driven to, you will find a way to learn. Find the books and people to teach you what you want to know how to do.

Creativity

Do you know people who are very creative?

What do they do?

It is likely you will discover they know how to daydream and they make time to relax out of the structured environment in which they work. Creativity is a process of unfolding layers of concepts or designs, and it begs for time, effort, and connecting the dots between ideas.

What triggers you to feel creative, relaxed, and open-minded? Something that works for me every time is to get a huge stack of magazines and ask myself, "What do I want to create? If I waved a magic wand and this was exactly the way I wanted it to be, what would it look, sound, and be like? How would I know it was here now?" In the magazines, I'm looking for all types of pictures that represent what I want to create. The answer to the question begins to show up in the collage. I cut out pictures that appeal to me, that have a connection in some way, and I spread them out on my conference room table. This gets my creative right brain engaged and flowing. When I notice myself feeling light and joyful as I explore the images of what could be possible, I am in my creative mode! Then I go look at the thing, product, or issue I want to bring creativity to. Inevitably I see something new that I had not thought about previously.

A commitment to thinking about and focusing on a creative project every day for a week can yield new thinking and the next big idea. I've found if I focus on something for two hours and then walk away from it to do something else, ideas will pop up as I am in the shower, driving to a meeting, or on a walk. Then I return back to the project for another two hours, and this cycle goes on until the project is completed.

Have someone else who is very creative review your work and discuss ideas for next steps. Getting input, especially from someone with a different viewpoint, provides new ideas. A different perspective helps stretch the mind and helps people see other sides that weren't previously considered, which can enrich the outcome.

Kate Early and Mark Bilodeau are masterful coaches for Odyssey of the Mind (OM), a creative problem-solving competition that encourages young people to develop their creativity. Kate and Mark's teams perform so well that they have gone to the world finals three out of the five years they have been coaching together. Because my son was on their team, I have seen firsthand how they guide the creative process.

One of the most important aspects of OM is the "no outside assistance" rule. What this means is that adults are not allowed to provide ideas; they can only ask questions to help team members think about solving the problems. "The fact that I can't provide answers to problems is the first step in developing creativity," Kate tells me. "Team members know that they must rely solely on themselves or other team members in order to find solutions to problems. This means that I have to create a team environment where members feel comfortable expressing themselves, evaluating ideas, and hearing criticism. Initial conversations that I have with the team establish the ground rules for communicating and also affirm the need for different types of creative talent."

So what are the kinds of questions that Kate and Mark ask to encourage divergent thinking? According to Kate, there are different kinds of questions for different stages in the creative process. In the beginning stage, when what is needed is a free flow of ideas, Kate uses basic brainstorming techniques. At this stage it's important to ask questions that free the team from its assumptions. "Last year we had to create 'aircraft' that flew in six different ways. When they hear the word *aircraft*, team members lock onto the idea of an airplane. So in order to encourage the team to envision other ways of flying, I asked, 'Besides airplanes, what other kinds of objects fly?' Identifying assumptions and asking questions that free people from those assumptions are crucial steps in nurturing creative thinking." Sammy Micklus, the son of Dr. Sam Micklus, the founder of OM, in an interview described how important it is to frame problems in an open-ended way. He said that instead of asking how to build a better toothbrush, it's better to ask how to create a better way of cleaning teeth. This is an important concept for professionals who want to be innovative because how we frame a problem heavily influences how we think about it and what we see as solutions.

Once the team chooses an idea to develop and starts creating pieces of the solution, another important question to ask is, "Is that the best idea? Or is there a way to make that better?" Beginning ideas should be starting places, not ending places. Kate says she often brings in other teammates when asking this question, to get the fresh perspective of people who haven't been locked onto that particular problem.

It's also important to ask questions that encourage the use of imagination in problem solving. Kate says, "Too often I think there's a tendency to shut down imagination because it's not focused on practical solutions. This year the team had to design vehicles powered by mousetraps, and those vehicles had to perform certain challenges. One of the challenges was 'team created,' so members had to envision something creative for the vehicle to accomplish. They were stuck on this problem, so I invited them to go back to their childhood and remember the vehicles that fascinated them. Amid answers like 'buses' and 'cranes' also came responses like 'hovercraft' and 'Luke Skywalker's Land Speeder.' Tapping into their childhood imaginations opened up new pathways of thinking, and soon ideas for new vehicle designs started to take shape."

There will be obstacles and failures on the road to a successful solution. If there is a low level of frustration, Kate asks specific questions directly related to the problem at hand. But the most important question she says she asks, "especially when frustration is high, is, 'Is it time to take a break?' The brain is at its problem-solving best when it's relaxed, so it's important to give team members permission to stop and do something else—have a snack, take a walk, go play."

Kate's creativity building ideas have been an inspiration to me, and I love to share them with coaching clients who want to build this ability.

Customer Focus

Most of us have both internal and external customers in our business. Who are your customers?

The first step in building customer focus is to care about the customers. Why are these people or these companies your customers? What is the service they need or want from you? Are you passionate about this product or service? Be passionate about both your customers and your products and services, and determine how this mix serves your values. Perhaps it is that customers enable you to earn your living—the more customers, the more living. Or perhaps it is that solving complex problems rewards you (fulfills your theoretical values) and the customers bring you complex issues to address. Or maybe it is that you are passionate about making the world a better place one person at a time (fulfilling your social values). Connect your own values and workplace motivators to why serving customers is important.

Stop to hear what it is the customers want, what they are looking for, or what is in their best interests. This may not necessarily be the best for your organization, but it is important to hear it from the customers' point of view. Sometimes this means listening closely to customers' complaints. What are they asking for? It may sound like whining: "I do not like that the report does not come in color. Why can't you produce a report that looks good?" Inside that complaint is a gift to you! It is a request that could give you an innovative way to create a new product or add more revenue to your bottom line.

Ask yourself if there is a way you can exceed the customers' expectations by providing more value than they bargained for. It helps distinguish your company from others when you go the extra mile. Creating raving fans who will talk about how great you are is a way to gain visibility and credibility to grow your business. You may be thinking, "We already have enough business, and we can't keep up with the volume we have now! My department is dumped on all the time, and everyone here is working 50- to 70-hour weeks consistently, and we can't keep up." Realize this: you are a customer to someone who needs to hear that! Talk with your management if you realize you are not able to serve your internal customers by keeping promises, meeting deadlines, and being friendly to work with because everyone is stressed out. Collaborate with your own management to solve this internal customer service issue.

Review and make suggestions to maintain internal processes to meet the current and changing needs of your customers. That helps your organization become more flexible in delivering value as you meet and exceed the customers' expectations.

Decision Making

Begin developing this ability by making a list of the biggest or most important decisions you have made in your past. Consider how you approached making these decisions. Did you have a process? Did you compare options? Or did you just jump in spontaneously or impulsively without much evaluation? Look at your own decision-making pattern from your past experiences.

In *"Yes" or "No": The Guide to Better Decisions* by Spencer Johnson, he advises you to ask these questions each time you are faced with an important decision:

- Am I meeting the real need, informing myself of options, and thinking it through?

- Does my decision show that I am being honest with myself and trusting my intuition and that I deserve better?

When you are making a decision, thinking though your answers to these questions in a journal will save you a great deal of time and heartache.

First, identify the upcoming decisions that you want to make or have been told to make. Put them into a timeline with a priority order. Developing clarity on the types of decisions in front of you and the priority that they have saves time and energy and yields better outcomes as you look at the big picture.

Schedule time to identify resources that help you make a big decision, and collect relevant information that impacts what you are considering. Exploring your options and research can come from a variety of sources, including the Internet, books, articles, and dialogue with those who can contribute information. Use a variety of sources to explore options.

The evidence is clear that sleeping on it is the scientifically sound decision, and it is the right course of action for anyone facing a challenging quandary, according to Maarten Bos and Amy Cuddy, social psychologists who study human behavior and decision making and the authors of the *Harvard Business Review* article, "A Counter-Intuitive Approach to Making Complex Decisions." What is the best way to approach complex decisions, according to these experts? In the article, they recommend you do these three things:

1. *Take in all information.* Before you can make a decision, you need to have the information. We should use our conscious mind to gather and encode all the necessary facts pertaining to a decision. Usually, some options can already be discarded in this stage, options that clearly violate a "decision rule"—for instance, "This apartment costs twice as much as what I can afford."

2. *Sleep on it.* Now that you have all the necessary information, you need to process it. Because your conscious attention is limited, you should enlist the help of your unconscious. Conscious

processes often disturb unconscious processes, so you need to distract your conscious mind.

3. *Check the facts.* Your unconscious can process large amounts of information, but it is not as precise as conscious thought. There is no amount of distraction that will help you answer an arithmetic question. Therefore, after you have made a choice unconsciously, you should check the facts of your decision consciously. Does your decision do any (serious) damage? Attributes are often interdependent—the value of one attribute influences the value of another: do all the attributes of the choice, taken together, violate a decision rule?

I like to give myself a realistic deadline to make a decision—the more complex the situation, the more likely I will want to sleep on it for two or three days. Ask yourself, "How long do I really have before the decision will be made for me if I do not make it?" Make the decision for yourself before someone else makes it for you.

Diplomacy and Tact

Selecting the right words and actions to communicate with people so that you don't offend them or trigger their anger is diplomacy. It is the opposite of being blunt and saying whatever is on your mind at the moment.

What is being diplomatic to one person may be beating around the bush to another. Understanding people's preferred communication styles helps to define where the line is for people in conversations. High Dominant Style communicators prefer direct, clear, blunt conversation. They do not like people who are too mild or diplomatic because those traits make it hard for the Dominant Style communicators to interpret the meaning. High Influential Style communicators prefer making things look and feel positive. They will want to be diplomatic and show it by being kind, friendly, and outgoing. High Steady Style communicators will be the most naturally diplomatic in their conversations—they do not want to offend or anger anyone. Someone with a Dominant Style may accuse Steady Style types of beating around the bush. It is vital that you respect their approach to communication if you want to have a successful long-term relationship with people who have a Steady Style. Compliant-to-Standards Style communicators will be mature and composed, and they will not push emotions too hard; however, they may push the facts and data firmly. Dominant and Compliant-to-Standards Style communicators are often the ones who are told they need to be more diplomatic and tactful.

When you want to be diplomatic, take responsibility for getting your own needs met in a way that preserves the dignity and style of the other person. Maintain good eye contact while communicating your needs, wants, feelings, and opinions in an open, honest manner.

Emotional Intelligence

Emotional intelligence (EI) is one of my favorite topics. This is a foundational skill for anyone who wants to be a star performer. If I were designing the abilities index for an organization, EI skills would be at the top of the list.

Developing emotional intelligence requires two things:

1. Understanding that there are seven core emotions and being aware of which one you are currently experiencing
2. Using the five abilities of EI effectively:
   ○ Self-awareness
   ○ Self-regulation
   ○ Motivation
   ○ Social skills
   ○ Empathy

Let's explore each part. First is understanding and being able to identify the triggers and symptoms of each of the seven core emotions:

- Love
- Joy
- Hope
- Sadness
- Envy
- Anger
- Fear

What causes or triggers you to feel each emotion? What are the physical and mental symptoms that you are feeling for each one?

You may be surprised to learn that each of these seven emotional states has a different chemical marinade associated with it. For example, when we are feeling angry, there is more adrenalin and cortisol in our bodies.

We have our own unique emotions map. What triggers me to feel love—someone's bringing a new puppy into the office for a visit—may cause someone else to feel anger. I love puppies!

Each of the five abilities related to emotional intelligence requires a different focus.

Self-awareness requires us to know what we are feeling in the moment—now—and to allow that to inform but not control our actions. To develop self-awareness, ask yourself the question, "What am I feeling now?" Ask this question two to three times every day, and track your answers. Write down the emotion and the triggers and symptoms of the feeling. This is the best way to begin raising emotional intelligence.

Self-regulation is our ability to intentionally decide how we want to use an emotion and not be hijacked by the feeling. When self-regulation is high, we ask ourselves the question, "What would be the best way to use this emotion to inform my actions?" rather than being taken over by the emotion.

Motivation is our ability to use our natural talents, strengths, and interests to keep ourselves growing, learning, and moving forward. When our motivation is high, we accept assignments and roles that play to our strengths and enable us to continue developing at a pace that works for our own learning style.

Social skill is our ability to use emotional intelligence with a group or team and to keep the team focused on the goals and moving forward. When a team gets bogged down in political gunk or low morale, that is a signal that there is low social skill at play. When social skill is high, teams are more effective, and over time, they become high performing.

The fifth ability is empathy, and it is so important that it has earned its own heading. Please see the next heading for more details.

Developing emotional intelligence, like any skill, takes focus and time. The best way to develop emotional intelligence is to keep an EI journal for 30 to 60 days asking the question, "What am I feeling now?" three times each day at different intervals. One of my clients set the timer on his watch to beep three times each day at rotating hours. When he heard the beep, it reminded him to ask, "What am I feeling now?" He would note the feeling and the trigger that caused this feeling to emerge, and then he would describe the symptoms in his thinking, body, and behavior. By doing this, he was able to dramatically increase his emotional intelligence.

Dottie Brienza is the senior vice president of global talent management at Hilton Worldwide. She has said, "Coaching is an investment in high-potential talent. In order to get to the C suite, people have to have both a high intelligence quotient (IQ) and a high emotional intelligence quotient (EQ). Developing EQ is vital for growth into leadership."

Empathy

Empathy is the ability to identify and understand what another person or group may be feeling now. Our ability to appropriately acknowledge the other person's feelings is a demonstration of our empathy.

It helped me enormously to learn that there are seven core emotions:

- Love
- Joy
- Hope
- Sadness
- Envy
- Anger
- Fear

All the other words we use to describe emotions are symptoms of these feelings. If you are able to memorize the list of emotions, you can then ask yourself, "Which of the seven feelings is the person I am speaking with likely to be experiencing now? What causes me to think this?" Then you will be able to acknowledge that person's emotions. You might say, "It appears you are feeling angry. Would you help me to understand what crossed your boundaries so we can clean up the issue?" Or if someone appears to be afraid, you could say, "I get the sense you may be feeling afraid of this project because it requires you to deliver a presentation. Would you like to discuss this? Perhaps I could work with you on the presentation, and we could use it as an opportunity to develop a new ability for you."

The science of emotional intelligence confirms that people are profoundly influenced by the moods of those around them. Emotions are contagious. This has a neurological basis, making it a powerful force when people work together. As leaders, we are responsible for engaging our employees, and a great deal of this has to do with their emotional set point about their work.

Employees who leave a negative emotional wake behind them affect coworkers in a variety of ways, and none of them are good. Energy and enthusiasm can be drained, along with the potential for the team to collaborate effectively. In an increasingly global business climate that requires forward thinking, innovation, and creativity to remain competitive, it is vital to build high-performance teams that know how to process through stuck emotional spots. Empathy is the key to this. Processing people through stuck emotions requires empathy as the first step in creating a dialogue that inspires new feelings and actions.

The first chapter in *Conversations for Change: 12 Ways to Say It Right When It Matters Most* provides guidance on what to look for, how to build emotional intelligence, and how to use it in conversations.

Employee Development and Coaching

This book focuses on building this capability; however, here are a few more ideas to share when this is the area for development.

There are four types of professional coaches, and they vary in purpose and qualifications:

- *Feedback coaches:* They provide assessments, feedback, and a development plan.
- *Insight and accountability coaches:* They are trusted advisors who ask questions like, "How would it feel to live your ideal leadership role? What are you doing to make this happen?" They are not focused on building capabilities, but rather on being a sounding board against which you can explore your own thinking
- *Content coaches:* They focus on building specific skills.
- *Development partners or learning experts:* They do all of the above as needed.

Which ones of these are you currently able to do well?

Having a professional business coach is similar to having a coach in sports or music. Singers have voice coaches whom they work with through their entire careers. Golfers are also coached throughout their entire careers. If we expect to continue to improve our management and leadership abilities, we need unbiased, ongoing performance feedback. We want employees and leaders who are ready for the future needs of the organization, not just the day-to-day work that is being done now.

When we ask employees to develop their management or leadership style to be prepared for future opportunities, we need to support their growth by providing someone who can give the right kind of feedback. This role of developmental coaching is not a temporary role for a corporate leader. Professional golfers want to play for years and continue to perform well, so they have a long-term coach. Star athletes expect to have a coach throughout their performance years as athletes. They want feedback and accountability over the time they are playing as high performers. The same is true of most executive leaders. In the future, this will mean that the profession of executive coaching will likely evolve to provide guidance and listening on an ongoing, long-term basis.

According to Lindsey Anderson, professional development trainer at Merck & Co., "Having an executive coach who is outside your organization is very important. Some of the best insight I get about how to be effective in my organization comes from people who are outside and not enmeshed in the political dynamics going on in my department and organization. It is a nonthreatening relationship that enables powerful Aha moments to occur."

Rob Greenhalgh, director of global talent development at World Fuel, said, "Coaching is the right intervention whenever you want to move an organization to a leadership culture."

I'm often asked how long the coaching relationship needs to continue. The key issue: is there a purpose to the coaching that is adding value to the top performer and the business? If so, keep the coaching going indefinitely. Sometimes coaching is about reflecting on past learning and how best to use it now. For example, every five years in a career, people benefit from working with a coach who serves as a sounding board to help them reevaluate who they are and what their interests and dreams are now.

Ask the person being coached, "What do you see as the incentive in having a coach? What do you want to do differently, more of, or less of? Is the coach helping you to grow?" If the answers are yes, then the coaching is on track.

Teresa Ressel, CEO of USB Securities, shared that she has benefited from working with a personal coach and also a team coach. In looking at large numbers of people, she found that those who have been coached have more clarity about who they are and are able to make better decisions about where they will fit in best as the organization grows. They are not overly focused on numbers and measurements, which enables them to be more aware of people professionally and personally. Those who have been coached are more effective. They ask themselves, "Do I want to be doing this? Will this project be motivating for me? How long do I want to commit to this role?" If you do not want to do something, it shows.

Teresa prefers team coaching so that everyone on the same team moves and grows together with a common language. She has said that in a prior experience, someone was coached on her own without the team's going through the same experience. The coachee grew, but the team did not. The coachee felt like she had outgrown the group within a year. When you provide growth for the whole team, everyone grows together and the team wins.

On the other hand, one-on-one coaching can create advantages too. A year after people have worked with a coach one-on-one without their team, they are likely ready to be "repotted" into a new role so they can use their new capabilities with a new team. Taking the next step without the team will help the individual reveal his or her long-term potential—can he or she be effective in developing and leading multiple teams?

Terry Hogan is the director of executive development at Citigroup. While speaking at a conference, she shared that the top third of executives at Citi have access to coaches and assessments that enable them to understand their preferences and motivators. They use the just-in-time learning model when someone is in a stretch assignment or moving to leading a new team. At that time a coach is able to add lots of value.

Also, it is wise to give the people being coached the opportunity to select their own coach from two or three options. I serve in the coaching pool in many organizations and have worked with executives who selected me because they had the **option** to do so.

You may be wondering, "Wait a minute, why does the C level value coaching? Aren't they suppose to be great leaders already?" Most executives have been coached and have a coach who serves as an ongoing sounding board. The coach provides direct feedback that staff members may not feel comfortable providing.

In addition, it is useful for executives to have coaches so that they have role models for themselves for the coaching experience that they provide in their own organizations. "Research shows leaders who coach others are more productive and less stressed," according to David Rock, the author of *Personal Best*. When you are responsible for employee development and coaching, put the focus on the learners: show them how to become better learners! Show your employees how to learn so they are self-directed. See leaders as facilitators who reinforce and role model learning.

When hiring new employees for your own team, ask yourself this question: "Of all my applicants who have the skills needed for the basic job, who is the least *qualified*?" Notice I am asking you to consider the candidate who *is* qualified, just not highly or overqualified. That is the person who will be most engaged in learning and most willing to be coached to fit into your role and organization.

If coaching is only about performance, you are not building a learning culture. What values do you want to reinforce in your culture? What values do you want leaders to live, model, and inspire in others? How do you want that to impact the future of your business?

When employees say they want coaching, they mean they want someone to care about them, have compassion toward them, listen to them, and answer their questions. They want someone to help them explore and reflect. Often when executives say they want coaching for their employees, what they mean is they want the coach to tell the employees how to be better performers, to "hold their feet to the fire" and make them accountable, to show them what is not working and how to fix it, to fill in the missing gaps, and to make them learn. This view needs to shift so that coaching can be an effective part of building a learning culture for the whole organization. When coaching is a developmental reward instead of a fix-it punishment, you will see an organization shift to be engaged in shared learning.

Consider making "coachability" part of the management selection criteria in your organization. When managers demonstrate that they are coachable and want to learn from others, the rest of the organization can then also admit when they want to learn something new or perform at a higher level.

Christine Williams is the director of leadership development for systems engineering within the NASA Academy of Program, Project and Engineering Leadership (APPEL). She is focused on developing NASA's best and brightest. She told me they provide five types of coaching for people with high potential:

- Coaching one-on-one
- Peer coaching
- Group coaching
- In-the-moment coaching
- Transition coaching

Let's take a look at what the second of these, peer coaching, is like.

Peer Coaching Example

In meetings, Chris provides all of the team members with cards that she asks them to fill out, one for each of the other meeting attendees. The questions on the card include:

- One of the things that your insights in this meeting provided to me was _____.

- Something else that could have been helpful would be
  _____.

- I am grateful that you _____.

At the end of the meeting, there is time built in for a round of *speed coaching.* This means each person spends one to two minutes with every other person in the meeting, giving him or her the card he or she filled out about that individual. Team members are taught that all they may say is "thank you" when they receive their peer feedback. In other words, they may not make defensive comments as a reply. Instead, they can only take in the feedback, weigh it, and reflect on it.

With in-the-moment coaching, Christine suggests that coaches start by asking, "May I coach you on something?" If the answer is yes, then give the feedback directly and ask for what you want to see happen. Then do it again right there in the moment as a "retake or do-over" so that the person has a chance to practice what he or she was coached on.

Do you believe some people are uncoachable? How do you approach coaching the uncoachable? Professional coaches tend to hold the belief that if the coach determines what the uncoachable people value and if the coach connects to those goals, then even seemingly uncoachable people can be coached! When people seem uncoachable, it is because the interaction their coach is having with them does not appear to them to match their current values and goals.

This book in your hands is the resource for developing this ability!

Flexibility

Brett M. Saks, vice president, human resources, for kgb USA, shared, "It has been my experience that a difficult skill to teach is *flexibility,* also described as *navigating organizational ambiguity.* Most would probably agree that as organizations become more matrixed and complex, the need for flexibility and ease with ambiguity is inevitable. Adding to the challenge is the fact that managers are often stretched so thin, especially in lean economic climates, that they have to act as part-time individual contributors and part-time managers (the proverbial player/coaches). This results in managers' having less time (or taking less time) to provide clear and specific directions, leaving their employees to simply 'figure it out.' Those who can be flexible with ambiguity, thrive. Those who cannot be flexible run the risk of being viewed as 'high maintenance' or 'overpaid' because they frequently need to be told what to do. Arguably, organizations could design clever business simulations or engage in ongoing structured role-plays in a classroom environment to help employees build flexibility in dealing with ambiguity, but that would require a lot of time and coordination.

"A more practical approach is to identify flexibility and ambiguity as cultural norms for all employees and then encourage managers to bring employees into situations in which the unknown is being navigated and managed openly. This comes through deliberate and intentional discussion by managers with their employees, and admittedly it requires discipline, but the payoffs can be enormous. Imagine an organization of young leaders who have learned how to manage the unknown from those who have succeeded and/or failed (which often yields even *more* learning) by managing the unknown by doing it alone. That is a culture to which we all need to aspire to build."

To maintain flexibility and to be able to deal with ambiguity, it's good to look for ways to be innovative with your project, role or team, and responsibilities:

- **Listen to the ideas of others.** Listening to feedback from others can give you insight into new and different channels you may not have considered. After you have listened to others, let yourself be influenced by your own ideas and intuition.

- **Be curious.** Change is the way of business, and you will eventually be required to adapt because no industry remains static. If you learn to develop your flexibility "muscle," you will be better prepared to deal with the inevitably of future change requirements.
- In *The Art of Non-Conformity*, Chris Guillebeau role models flexibility and dealing with ambiguity as he shares his own life experiences.
- A resource for more flexible conversations is my book *Conversations for Change: 12 Ways to Say It Right When It Matters Most*.

Futuristic Thinking

This is the rarest of the 24 capabilities on this list. When you find people who have mastered this ability, hang on to them!

Have you ever watched a movie like *Back to the Future II* and wondered what life will be like in the future? Intentionally thinking about what business trends will impact your industry, your company, or the world is an example of futuristic thinking.

Flash Foresight: How to See the Invisible and Do the Impossible, written by futurist Dan Burrus, describes seven radical principles that let you see into the future. Dan defines *flash foresight* as a "sudden burst of insight about the future that produces a new and radically different way of doing something that will open up invisible opportunities and solve seemingly impossible problems before they happen." The seven radical actions that guide the way to seeing the future are these:

Start with Certainty

In an uncertain world, ask, "What am I certain about?" A strategy based on certainty has low risk and high reward. Hard trends will happen; soft trends might happen. After winter comes spring—a simple example of a hard trend.

Anticipate

We are all crisis managers, managing change from the outside in, putting out fires. We need to use hard trends to become anticipatory based on what we do know will happen.

Transform

Technology is transforming how we sell, market, communicate, collaborate, train, educate, and innovate in a very short amount of time. If you are only changing those things, you will fail!

Take Your Biggest Problem—and Skip It

The reason you can't solve your big problems is the fact that they are not the real problems; they are the perceived problems. By skipping what you think the problem is, you can quickly find the real problem and solve it.

Go Opposite

Opposites work better. The opposite of an expensive leather shoe is a cheap rubber shoe: Crocs shoes and sandals did quite well.

Redefine and Reinvent

Technology-driven transformation will happen whether you like it or not. The way to thrive is to use transformation to redefine and reinvent your career as well as your business.

Direct Your Future

Instead of letting the future unfold and living on hope for a better tomorrow, use the forces of predictable change to shape a better future for yourself and others.

Read Dan's book, and check out www.burrus.com/about-dan/ for more guidance on developing this ability.

Goal Achievement

Your current life is like a display case for your past goals. Think about that for a moment. Look around your office and home and notice that these places are displaying the results of your past goals. This was clear to me after several things happened in the same week: the arrival of bedroom furniture that had been on order for four months, the acceptance into a private organization I had wanted to be a member of, and my reaching my desired number on the scale. All of these things happened because I was clear on wanting them, and I took the actions necessary to produce the desired results.

As a manager and coach, you will need to inspire your team members to set and deliver on goals. This is a conversation you'll need to create with your team members. I've written the following paragraphs in the way you might speak to your employees or team members so as to give you the language you'll need to make it easy for you to coach and train people in developing this vital skill.

You need to know how to establish and deliver on your goals. Are you creating your work by setting goals? Or are you deferring the creative effort for defining your goals to other people, deferring instead to their agenda in a reactive way?

Accept responsibility for your own career by understanding that everything that happens to you is a result of your decision to take responsibility for yourself or defer it to others. What matters is where you are going, not where you have been. Put your hands on the steering wheel of your own life by creating your career goals based on your own interests and talents. Be the predominant creative force in your own life!

So many organizations believe that past performance determines future performance. That is not always the case! There is much change going on in the world today, and it is very clear that people who were successful selling door to door or in person in the past will not necessarily make it in other types of selling situations if they do not change their way of selling. What caused us to win last year may not cause us to win this year. Awareness of the current reality is vital to create goals that will lead people to successful outcomes.

The author of *Goals!* Brian Tracy, says, "The ability to set goals and to make plans for their achievement is what leads to sustainable long-term success." You can learn what you need to learn to achieve your goals. This is very inspiring when someone accepts this as the truth. Dedicate yourself to life-long learning that aligns with your goals. Once you meet a goal, move forward to another one.

Decide exactly what you want in your life and work. Write it down:

- What activities each day will you need to engage in to achieve those goals?
- What do you need to be excellent at doing in order to bring your goals to life?

Write down your three to five most important goals in life right now. (You have 30 seconds to answer this question now.) This gives you a quick snapshot of what is most important to you.

Now look at each goal and rewrite it so that it is clear, specific, detailed, and measurable, as if you were placing an order with a builder. Would a contractor be able to deliver it to you if he or she read your goal?

Identify the obstacles to be overcome. Of all the obstacles you have to overcome, which is the most important? What is the limiting factor? Most constraints are internal limitations, not external. Is your limiting factor that you need to develop a skill, better habits, or a new way of thinking? Concentrate on breaking through the limitation. Vet this with other people to see if they see it the way you do.

Our weakest skill establishes the height of our income. Developing that one skill will dramatically increase the quality of our lives. This may not be obvious to everyone, but it is the truth: every skill is learnable. When you focus on a specific skill and want to master it, realize that if you focus, you will be able to achieve the expert level in five years or 10,000 hours of practice. Once you master a skill, then select another one you want to master and focus on it. You can do this again and again. When you do this, you will see your income and your ability to make a positive difference in the world increase dramatically.

Identify the people who could help you reach your goals. Help the people around you to understand your goals. Ask people for specific actions you could take that would enable you to move forward in reaching your goal. Also, show other people how you could assist them. Create these conversations with everyone in your life. Some people talk about other people (gossip), some people talk about events, but it is the people who talk about their and others' goals that move the world forward.

Make a list of everything you need to do to accomplish the goal. Add to the list as you see new things that you want to do to meet your goal. Then organize this list by priority and by sequence. What is the first step that you will need to take? Focus on the critical actions that will make the most difference.

Make a plan. What is the first step you will take? Then what? And then what?

Plan your life around your goals. Have you ever heard the old saying, "Proper and prior planning prevents poor performance"? Each year, month, and week, create a plan that aligns with your goals in advance. Look at your goals first, and then ask what actions you need to take today to move toward them. Every minute you spend in planning will save you at least 10 minutes in execution.

Make a list of what you need to do each day. Ask, "What one thing do I need to do first today? What is the second thing I need to do today?" Discipline yourself to work on your number one task until it is completed. If you begin a major task and you stop it before you are finished, it takes you far more time to get restarted. It takes five times as long to complete a task if you allow interruptions and have to figure out where you were. This is counterintuitive for people who are jumping around with multiple software programs open and e-mail and text messages beeping while they are listening to a team meeting on the phone. Focus on one thing at a time, complete it, and then move to the next.

Visualize the outcomes completed. The ability to imagine is one of the most powerful abilities you have. See what you want to Be, Do, Then Have regularly. The greater clarity you have, the faster you will achieve the goal. The fuzzier you are about the goal, the longer it will take to achieve. Imagine what the goal would look like if it were attained. Create a picture of what you want, and look at it regularly. Feed your mind this picture over and over, and watch amazing things happen. This works for short-term and long-term goals. Imagine the feeling you will have when you have accomplished the outcomes. Create the emotion that would go along with that picture. Do this daily until you have achieved the desired outcome. I have a bulletin board in front of my desk that has pictures of what I want to create hanging in front of me so I am reminded all day of what my top goals are. I see them as if they are already accomplished, and that keeps my momentum going so that I take the next action needed to achieve them.

Go get a blank sheet of paper now, and write 10 goals using the format below. Write in the present tense as if it were already a reality. Write it the way you want it exactly. State what you do want, not what you do not want:

> The format is "I" plus an action verb—for example, "I own my dream home," "I exceeded my sales goal for this year." or "I eat pure nutritious food."

Look over the list of your goals. Pick the **one** that would have the greatest impact on your life now. Decide which one you want to be your major definite purpose for now. This goal is the one you will work on and think about every day until it is accomplished. Do something every day, seven days per week, that moves you closer to the goal—even if that action consists of only visualizing yourself celebrating the successful outcome. Once you have reached it, celebrate. Then move on to the next goal.

Use your learning journal. Write your goals every day, and you will see amazing results happening in the next 30, 60, and in 90 days. You will be feeling grateful that you took these actions.

Do you want more content that will enable you to focus on the right actions to develop goal achievement abilities? Read *Goals! How to Get Everything You Want Faster Than You Ever Thought Possible* by Brian Tracy, and check out www.Brian Tracy.com.

Interpersonal Skills

At a recent executive coaching conference in New York City, I met the person at NASA who heads leadership development for rocket scientists. She told me, "The people side of our work is more complex than the technical side of our work. We are all systems engineers. The systems we work in are human systems, which are infinitely more complex than anything else we do." This means that understanding human interaction or interpersonal skills is more challenging than being a rocket scientist!

People reading is the skill I use to understand human behavior and motivators. What causes a person to do what he or she does, what is predicable, and how can we be more effective in communicating with all people? Understanding workplace motivators and preferred communication styles is the first step in people reading. In my previous book *Conversations for Change,* you will find in Chapters 2 and 3 an overview of workplace motivators and communication styles. Reading those chapters and having that know-how is the first step in developing interpersonal skill awareness. My blog www.ShawnKentHayashi.com also provides specifics to show you how to read people.

People reading takes practice. If you want to be really good at identifying other people's motivators and communication styles, focus on reading someone new every day for the next 60 days. Ask, "Is this person being more task focused or people focused? Does this person prefer a faster pace and quick decision making or a more methodical approach and at least three days to make a significant decision?" The answers to these questions will help you identify the other person's communication style preferences. What causes the people you are reading to feel passionate or engaged? The answer will point you to their motivators.

People reading is one of the most interesting and entertaining things you can do. We are all different; however, once you learn what to look for and how to connect with others in meaningful ways based on people's motivators and communication styles, you will feel confident to talk with anyone—even rocket scientists!

"You can get everything you want in life by helping others get what they want," according to Zig Ziglar. So how do you identify what the other people want? Understand their preferred communication style and how it impacts their needs. Our preferred communication style will indicate what we need. Have you noticed some people have more of some of these traits than others?

- Forceful, direct, and results oriented
- Optimistic, fun, and talkative
- Steady, patient, and relaxed
- Precise, accurate, and detail oriented

And some people have combinations of two or three of these patterns?

A person who understands other people and what they need in communication is well respected and able to make contributions that better the lives of others.

DISC (dominance, influence, steadiness, conscientiousness) analysis is based on the universal language of observable human behavior and thus preferred communication styles. Watching people proves its validity. Every day we live in a wonderful laboratory where we can observe or read people. Scientific research has proven that people, in terms of how they act, have similar patterns of behavior or characteristics. By learning these characteristics, we can increase communication effectiveness.

DISC does not measure intelligence, values, skills, experience, or education and training. But, yes, our DISC style has an inescapable influence on all of these.

If you would like to discover your preferred communication style, complete the online assessment, and/or read the book *The Universal Language DISC* by Bill J. Bonnstetter, Judy I. Suiter, and Randy J. Widrick. You will find both here: www.theprofessional developmentgroup.com/online-store/.

Leadership

In *CEO Material: How to Be a Leader in Any Organization* (McGraw-Hill, 2009), the *New York Times* best-selling author D. A. Benton asks, "What does being a leader look like?" She immediately answers the question with the following:

If you choose to lead (because it is your choice), you:

- Think "we" instead of "me"; you put forth individual effort to create team-based wins.
- Have other awareness, not just self-awareness, and you campaign for others, not just yourself.
- Understand that being a leader is a service job—service to employees, social causes, and customers.
- Improve your people's reputations, not just your own, and you keep it about others, not about you.
- Grow others and share credit; you make it possible for others to use their abilities, and you take people to places they normally wouldn't go on their own.
- Don't just focus on your work but focus instead on the business as a whole; you get a large number of people moving in a similar direction where they're able to accomplish a great thing.

- Build a team of like-minded people around you and fill in gaps of what is missing in your own expertise.
- Take responsibility for your own weaknesses, even if only in private, and you put people around you with those skills.
- Grow things and free up capital, and you see where the company can go and where you can be of help.
- Keep whatever team you lead moving.
- Do more than get everything done; make a huge impact everyday.
- Spark ambition in others—both those under your direct control and those who aren't.
- Make choices, minute by minute, that make you better in your work.
- Treat your people as associates and colleagues, not subordinates.
- Have organized thinking, and you can take a problem or opportunity and sort it out logically.

A CEO recently shared with me that her team had confronted her directly in a meeting. They told her they did not think she understood the reality that they were facing and the workloads that their teams had been living with. At first she was shocked, but she kept listening and asking questions to understand. Afterward she told me, "If you are in leadership, you may think you really understand how the organization and positions within it work and what your employees do. Yet, the reality is that there has been so much change in the past few years, and most roles have changed dramatically. We may not really understand the impact of this on people and their performance now. When employees say that they are overwhelmed and that the leadership does not know what they are doing or how much work they have responsibility for, listen. Ask questions and observe what really is happening now in your organization because your people are your most important assets. If you ignore this, you are not leading your people."

One of my client organizations has given a department so much work that the managers have been working 60- to

70-hour weeks for months on end. This is burning out the employees, who have now lost their creativity and resourcefulness, and are just trying to keep up. Several managers in this department have indicated to me that they are now looking for a new position in another organization where there are realistic workloads. They have lost trust in their leadership to hear their issues and work collaboratively to solve problems. As a leader, don't make this mistake yourself.

Negotiation

Like it or not, everyone negotiates every day! In all aspects of life, we are constantly negotiating. Especially in the workplace, we are continually called upon to successfully negotiate with customers, coworkers, supervisors, and internal support personnel. Often, our approach to conflict resolution is influenced by a competitive win-lose approach when what we need is to foster successful long-term relationships by creating win-win outcomes. It is useful to examine your own beliefs and practices about negotiating so that you will become more effective the next time you find yourself needing to make your point or get your way.

Negotiation is a basic means of getting what you want from others. Negotiation is the process we use to deal with our differences. When we find ourselves faced with any type of negotiation, remember this:

Understand the distinction between selling and negotiating. Sell the merits of the whole package or offering before beginning to make changes to any single piece.

Here are some basic tips:

- Know when to begin negotiating.
- Utilize a wide variety of options in creating an agreement. Most of us do not think enough about the available

alternatives; instead, we go with the first idea that pops into our heads.

- Evaluate your process of negotiating; think through the whole cycle of planning and conducting the conversations that will help you secure a long-term relationship.
- Negotiating begins with knowing what you want. Think of two things, situations, or experiences you want—things about which you will probably have to interact with others in order to have or get. Once you are clear about what you want, you can begin using your influence skills to get it.
- Even the most influential and the most astute negotiators make mistakes when stress is high. Being clear about what can go wrong in a negotiation can help you avoid the common pitfalls.

What Goes Wrong in Negotiations?

Here are some negotiation actions to avoid:

- Negotiating too soon, that is, agreeing to a price before you have heard all the needs and objections.
- Negotiating too much. Agreeing to change too many aspects of your proposal so that the final agreement does not meet your own needs.
- Negotiating under an ultimatum, that is, having to make a decision with too little time to obtain all the information you need to prepare.
- Not thinking win-win in long-term relationships. Or thinking win-win in a one-time negotiation relationship.
- The other parties use bluffing techniques or delays as tactics or say they are ready to buy when they really aren't.
- The clients don't know what they need, and they have no criteria to evaluate the success of the deal.
- Ethical or legal problems, that is, dealing with someone from a country where bribes are standard practice.
- Not being clear on what you want, what your *best alternative to a negotiated agreement* (BATNA) is, or what you

will do if you do not do this. The idea of a BATNA comes from *Getting to Yes* by Roger Fisher and William Ury—this series of books is the best on negotiations I've read.

When to Use the Negotiation Options

Here is a guide for choosing when to use the negotiation options:

Option and Definition	When to Use
Trade: Involves two variables like cost and delivery time.	Your first choice—best alternative.
Give away: You add something of value to the customer that doesn't cost you much.	You have no flexibility in the package you have offered.
Split the difference: Focusing on one variable, both parties give in some; does not have to be an equal split.	Unimportant difference can get discussions moving.
Concession: Giving in on one variable.	Trivial difference.
Walk away: Stop the negotiation because one of the parties will not win.	Your BATNA is stronger than the negotiated agreement, if one or more parties will lose.

All too often people simply adopt the most obvious position without spending the time to think through all the possible alternatives. Prior to any negotiation, use the chart to trigger you to create at least three options. You will have more to offer in the conversation if you have done your homework first. When you apply these ideas in your negotiations, you can face your daily negotiations with confidence and reap the rewards of long-term relationships based on win-win agreements.

Jane Dolente is the managing principal of The Skilled Negotiator (www.TheSkilledNegotiator.com), and she shared this story with me:

One of the famous rules in negotiations is to focus on interests, not positions. I taught this rule countless times, so I was shocked to find myself in the middle of a heated argument with my husband about—you guessed it—POSITIONS!

Every night I had to squeeze out of my car, Houdini style, because a roll of discarded carpet blocked my door. I was fed up. I burst into the house and announced, "Tomorrow, that rug goes!" My husband of course responded with his position, "That rug stays!" Back and forth we went until I wondered, what if one of my clients overheard this conversation? I would be found out as a total fraud.

I took a breath and started over. By asking questions and listening, behaviors that separate great negotiators from average ones, I found out that my husband hated waste. We had paid over $1,800 for that carpet, but we had pulled it up after only six months of wear and replaced it with ceramic tile. The high traffic pattern in the room plus the pale blue color was a lethal combination. Despite the wear, my husband believed that the rug still had some value. Giving it away made no sense to him. His interests were not to throw away valuables. My interests were to get the clutter out of the garage. The conversation about interests enabled us to come up with a perfect solution. We cut out the stained portions and put the remaining two smaller carpet pieces in the basement to spruce up our fitness center. The next time you are locked in conflict, try asking questions to discover the other side's interests. A creative solution often follows.

Persuasion

How do you help someone else to see your point of view? What you use to have someone come to agree with you is *persuasion*.

What is considered "persuasive" by one person can turn someone else off. Therefore, the better you understand communication styles, the more persuasive you will be able to be.

Dominant Style communicators will be persuaded by competence, direct language, and big-picture thinking that inspires a decision to be made now. They love a challenge that needs to be tackled full steam ahead, so present your idea to appeal to this reality. Be brief, bold, and to the point. Stick to business.

Influential Style communicators will be persuaded by social proof—seeing that others they respect are doing it too and feeling excited. They love new trends and opportunities, so position your ideas highlighting what will appeal to their style. Use an emotional appeal to get their attention. Be friendly and willing to talk socially.

Steady Style communicators will be persuaded by seeing the process step by step. They will want time to think it through for themselves, so do not push them to make a decision. They do not like change, so help them to see how the idea builds on something they are already doing. Tell them that the change will be available in a pilot version or draft form so they can experience it from beginning to end before they commit long term. Be friendly and relaxed.

Compliant-to-Standards Style communicators will be persuaded by facts, data, and logic. They want to review the research before they will agree. Do not use emotional appeals to persuade them. If you are patient with their questions, it is more likely that they will see your point of view. Stick to business.

If you would like to discover your preferred communication style, complete the online assessment and/or read the book *The Universal Language DISC* by Bill J. Bonnstetter, Judy I. Suiter, and Randy J. Widrick. You will find both here: www.theprofessional developmentgroup.com/online-store/.

Practice identifying people's communication styles, which I call *people reading*, and ask yourself, "How would I approach persuading that person?" Follow up by checking out the resources at www.ShawnKentHayashi.com.

Planning and Organization

My personal philosophy on organizing is this three-step process:

* Keep only what you love and will use.
* Have a place for everything.
* Keep everything in its place.

Keeping only what you love requires that you go through your possessions and schedule and release what you no longer love. If a file folder, chair, or picture on the wall does not represent you, let it go. If you can't say, "I love that!" then donate it to someone who would appreciate it so you have space for new things that you do love. This works in your office, calendar, closet, or anywhere you go. To prove this to yourself, choose one area, go through each item—everything—and ask yourself the question, "Do I love using this? Do I want to keep it?" What you can't answer yes to, place in a donation or trash pile and let it go. Or delete it from your schedule if it is a repeating meeting that you realize is no longer adding value.

Having a place for everything also applies to your space, computer storage, and schedule—everything you own. In my office I have a place for pens, tape, scissors, financial files, books to read, and books I've already read. Just as every item has a place in a kitchen, each item in my office has its own place. On my laptop I have a place for my schedule, client folders, budget, and every other chunk of my business and personal life. Having a place in the schedule for exercising, team meetings, and family dinners is an example of how this principle applies to your schedule.

Create a system for yourself to return things to their space. Just as you do with the dishwasher in the kitchen when the dishes are clean, you put them away where they belong. Friday afternoons is my time to return things to their space and clean out my e-mail in-box—if something interferes with this on Friday afternoon, then I move that three-hour chunk of time to another space in my schedule. This ritual is vital to keeping the planning and organizing system working.

David Allen is the guru and author of *Getting Things Done*. I highly recommend reading his book for two reasons. First, he shows you a system for planning and organizing that works anywhere you go. Second, once you use the system faithfully, your life will be transformed—you will be able to relax when you want to relax because you know that the things that need to be done will be done because you put them into your system. I learned to keep a single list of everything I commit to doing—

one ongoing list. I use a bound journal, and in it I write down everything I agree to do, need to do, or want to do. This is my ongoing project list. Referencing it daily and reviewing the whole list every Friday is part of my system to stay focused on the plan and organized.

> The Primary reason for failure is that people do not develop new plans to replace those plans that didn't work.
>
> —Napoleon Hill

If you are managing someone with a high Influential Communication Style, he or she will need guidance in planning and organizing. Lora has a high Influential Communication Style: she is very charming, people gravitate to her, and she loves interacting with all types of people. However, creating structures that enable her to meet her own goals and organizing her space and time have been long-time issues for her. When I began working with Lora, she was already a star performer in sales—she had won many awards for outstanding achievements in her organization.

Nevertheless, her home office was filled waist high with papers and brochures, and her time schedule was scattered. It was costing her time as she tried to find things, which slowed her down. "When you keep only what you love, it is much easier to make decisions. I feel so much better about myself and my own ability to change the things I do not want in my life," Lora said to me after we organized her space. This is a new way of thinking for Lora. She needed the confidence and accountability to make a change. She also told me that her success was due in part to hearing me say, "You have done this before, Lora. You know where everything is in your kitchen, right? You have what it takes to do this too!"

Once you have created structures for success, you can confront what does not work. Organization does not happen overnight. It is a process, a shift in your way of thinking. You have small wins when you learn to keep a drawer or a room organized. You stop operating from a place of fear, which arises when you are in a disorganized space.

Planning is about creating the structure to bring your goals alive, and it requires that you are organized in your thinking. What are the next steps that need to occur to move this project forward? What does the desired outcome look like? Who knows how to accomplish what you want done? Would you be willing ask them if they would share their advice or action plan with you?

Presenting

The ability to present your ideas and to successfully persuade others is vital for developing star performers. The people you manage will need you to both role model and teach them presentation skills. You can teach them how to do so by using the ideas given here.

There are two aspects of presenting: designing a presentation that will connect with your audience and then delivering it confidently. When you know you have a presentation coming up, ask yourself these questions:

- What does the audience want to know?
- Is my purpose primarily to persuade, inform, or entertain?
- What are the three to five key concepts or ideas that are most important?
- How could I structure my material into three to five key buckets and provide the stories, data, facts, and information needed in each of these areas?

The body of your presentation is created by the answers to the questions above. It will include facts, data, stories, and examples that bring your points alive. The body of the presentation would be about 80 percent of the time you are speaking.

After you are clear on this, then you'll design the opening and the conclusion.

The opening needs to include four parts:

- *A grabber that gets their attention:* This could be a story, question, or fascinating statistic. It must relate to your key message.
- *What's in it for the audience:* Why should they care about your message?
- *Why I'm speaking on this topic:* What gives you the ability to deliver this message?
- *A preview of the presentation:* Tell them what you are going to be telling them—your central theme.

The conclusion needs three parts:

- *A summary of your key points.*
- *An opportunity to answer questions:* A great way for you to showcase how much you know about your topic is by being open to all questions. It is my favorite part of delivering a presentation because it is where I can seal the deal in connecting with my audience.
- *Your final words:* Perhaps a story or quote that ties everything together.

Then practice, practice, practice. Practice out loud, imagining the audience in front of you. Say the presentation out loud while you are in the shower, driving to work, exercising—by saying the presentation out loud at least seven times, you will be able to confidently stand and deliver when the time comes to be a star presenter.

A book that will take this deeper is *Power Presentations: How to Connect with Your Audience and Sell Your Ideas* by Marjorie Brody and Shawn Kent.

Problem Solving

People with high Theoretical motivators and/or values love problem solving. Do you know people who are masterful at problem solving? What do they do?

Tim Hicks is a mediator who currently directs and teaches problem solving in the master's degree program at the University of Oregon. With permission, here are Tim's seven steps for problem solving.

Step 1. Identify the Issues
- Be clear about what the problem is.
- Remember that different people might have different views of what the issues are.
- *Separate the listing of issues from the identification of interests (that's the next step!).*

Step 2. Understand Everyone's Interests
- This is a critical step that is usually missing.
- Interests are the needs that you want satisfied by any given solution. We often ignore our true interests as we become attached to one particular solution.
- The best solution is the one that satisfies everyone's interests.
- This is the time for active listening. Put down your differences for a while, and listen to each other with the intention to understand.
- *Separate the naming of interests from the listing of solutions.*

Step 3. List the Possible Solutions (Options)
- This is the time to do some brainstorming.
- There may be lots of room for creativity.
- *Separate the listing of options from the evaluation of the options.*

Step 4. Evaluate the Options
- What are the positive and negative aspects?
- *Separate the evaluation of options from the selection of options.*

Step 5. Select an Option or Options
- What's the best option, in the balance?
- Is there a way to "bundle" a number of options together for a more satisfactory solution?

Step 6. Document the Agreements
- Don't rely on memory.
- Writing it down will help you think through all the details and implications.

Step 7. Agree on Contingencies, Monitoring, and Evaluation
- Conditions may change. Make contingency agreements about foreseeable future circumstances (if-then!).
- How will you monitor compliance and follow-through?

Effective problem solving does take time, but it takes less time and attention than is required by a problem that was not well solved. What it really takes is the willingness to slow down. A problem is like a curve in the road. Take it right and you'll find yourself in good shape for the straightaway that follows. Take it too fast and you may not be in as good shape.

Working through this process is not always a linear exercise. You may have to cycle back to an earlier step. For example, if you're having trouble selecting an option, you may have to go back to thinking about the interests. This process can be used in a large group, between two people, or by one person who is faced with a difficult decision. The more difficult and important the problem, the more helpful and necessary it is to use a disciplined process. If you're just trying to decide which movie to see, you don't need to go through these seven steps! Don't worry if it feels a bit unfamiliar and uncomfortable at first. You'll have lots of opportunities to practice.

The game Master Mind teaches the thinking skills needed in problem solving. I've been known to play it during lunch hours with employees, during interviews with candidates for roles that require complex problem solving, or during coaching sessions with people who want to develop problem solving ability. I put four different-colored pegs into the code, and then the clients begin to solve the problem. Give it a try, and you will see how this develops your ability in problem solving.

Resiliency

Sophia had been a star performer in her organization consistently over a five-year period. Several times she had been the top-performing salesperson nationally in her organization. She was referred to me as a coach because she was a stuck star. Three years earlier, Sophia had been engaged to the love of her life. Three weeks before the wedding, in his midthirties, her fiancé died of a heart attack. This is a very sad life experience. Sophia's life changed course in a moment. She did not.

Her boss, Noah, knew she had what it takes to be in the top-performing sales range again. He just was not sure how to help Sophia regain her own focus and drive. Noah asked Sophia if she would like to work with a coach, since several other leaders in their organization were doing the same. When Noah called me, he did not mention that Sophia's fiancé had died three years earlier. Instead, he told me about her past accomplishments in the sales organization and how focused and driven she used to be and that he could not seem to help her now. The first time I met with Sophia, I asked her to tell me about herself.

Sophia immediately talked about having been engaged and how painful it was that her fiancé had died. She told me about the things she and her fiancé did the day before he died, about the clothes he wore and the way he talked, about his favorite foods. She told me about every gift she had ever given him. I listened attentively to details about her fiancé and the wedding that never happened for over 30 minutes. I asked Sophia how long ago this had happened, thinking it had been a few weeks ago. When she said it had been three years ago, I asked what she had been doing in the past year. She did not have much of an answer—there were no new accomplishments to report.

When I asked questions about her goals for the future, she did not have much of an answer. She returned to telling me about her fiancé's dreams and what they had planned to do together. That is when I realized that Sophia was stuck in this emotional groove. Her emotional set point was on sadness, and she was not budging.

I said, "Sophia, over the next week between our meetings, would you be willing to focus on what you want to create for yourself now? Would you be willing to explore what you want the story of your life to be? Sophia, I understand what happened to you was very sad, and you may make that the story of your life, if you would like to do so. Or you may decide you want to create another story for your life. I have been through terrible life experiences like losing a baby at seven months and having a dear friend die unexpectedly, and I also know others who have experienced tragedies such as having terrible legal battles with a former spouse or business partner and losing their children or their entire business, or living through the loss of their family and everything they owned due to a tsunami. These losses are deeply sad. But they do not have to be the final chapter in the story that is retold every time we think of that person. All of the people who came to mind for me as I mentioned those examples have gone on in their lives to build something that they are proud of, and they also have found a way to move forward instead of staying stuck in sadness. I had to let go of the dreams I had for the child that died in order to move on. Would you be willing to do that too? Would you be willing to create some new pictures of where you would like your career and your life to go from here?"

Sophia said she would be willing.

Over the next three months, Sophia and I talked through her goals for the future. She reconnected with feelings of hope, joy, and love instead of retelling herself that something very sad had happened to her. Sophia set new goals to be in the top sales categories again. This was not an issue of building technical skills or know-how. It was about helping her to be emotionally intelligent so that she could be resilient. She told me at our final coaching meeting that the most powerful comment I had made to her that shifted everything was: "You do not have to make that experience the story of your life. You can create a new path that honors the past and yet gives you hope and love."

The key to resilient behavior is realizing that you have choices about what the story of your life is. Do the best you can with what you have and then move on.

Want to read a book that will help you develop resilience? Try *Optimal Thinking: How to Be Your Best Self* by Dr. Rosalene Glickman or *The Resilience Factor: 7 Keys to Finding Your Inner Strength and Overcoming Life's Hurdles* by Karen Reivich, PhD, and Andrew Shatté, PhD.

Self-Management

If you want to develop star performers, you will have to be able to self-manage and you will have to be in peak condition yourself in order to gain their trust and respect. When we think about this topic, we are considering such actions as dieting, budgeting money, and creating a time management log. The discipline to do what we say we are going to do is what self-management is all about. This ability is also demonstrated in emotional intelligence when we refer to *self-regulation*. Our ability to use our emotions consciously, intentionally, and without going into an emotional hijack is determined by our self-management. Knowing where you are, knowing what you need and want, and then working the plan to get there requires self-management.

When you stand on the scale, do you weigh what you want to weigh? If so, you are applying this skill. This is an issue of self-management.

Do you have a personal spending plan that enables you to allocate your money and resources to meet your goals? Do you have savings that equate to your age and place in life? Do you faithfully save 10 percent of your income in your 401(k)? If so, you are someone who has strong self-management ability, and you are applying it to your finances.

Do you use your time wisely, effectively saying yes to what needs to be done and no to what needs to be let go? If so, this is another sign that you are someone who has strong self-management ability, and you are using it focused on time.

These are examples of places where our self-management muscle or discipline ability speaks louder and clearer than our words. If these areas are not where you want them to be, it is time to build self-management skills. To do so, select one of the areas in which you want to make a difference.

If you do not weigh what you want to, read *No Flour, No Sugar* by Dr. Gott or *Cinch!* by Cynthia Sass. Both of these books will provide a plan that will give you the framework to practice building your self-management muscle as it relates to the number that shows up when you stand on the scale.

If you are in debt and you do not have the level of financial freedom that you want, read *Your Life or Your Money* by Vicki Robin. You will find a framework that you can use to build your self-management muscles focused on your finances.

Building self-discipline takes focus over at least a 30- to 90-day period. If this is the developmental area you are focused on, connect with a coach daily as an accountability buddy to keep you on track until you reach your desired goal. It is likely that you will need additional support to keep you focused until this muscle is very strong.

One of my favorite coaching clients, Emily, came to our first meeting telling me she wanted to be more influential in her business and industry. I was excited about working with her because she was clearly a star in her profession as a talent manager. Being more influential in her organization and in her industry was the key issue she wanted our coaching to focus on.

As our conversation evolved, she shared that she was unhappy with the 30 extra pounds she was carrying. A few paragraphs later, she mentioned she had $50,000 in credit card debt, which was limiting her ability to do some things she really wanted to do. She said she did not know how she was going to get out from under the enormous debt. A few paragraphs later, she said she did not feel that she managed her time well because she regularly did other people's work for them when her own was not completed. It became clear that her core issue—her weakest ability—was self-management. I knew that working on this one ability would positively transform Emily's life. I asked her if she was willing to develop self-management before we focused on her influence ability, since there would be a positive and significant spillover from developing this ability first. I said it was vital to the success of our work together in influence. Emily agreed.

We began with having her focus on losing the 30 pounds. Together we went to Whole Foods, and I showed her how to shop for and prepare healthy foods. She read the two books on eating plans I suggested, and we prepared several meals together. She learned how to prepare healthy food and make wise food choices when traveling. In the first 30 days she lost 12 pounds. This success gave her the momentum to be willing to then focus on creating a spending plan.

During the second month, I showed her how to create a spending plan the way a mentor of mine showed me many years ago. Emily began to track her spending, identified where she needed to cut expenses, and created a plan to pay off all her debt in three years. Each day she e-mailed me with what she had spent and where she had cut expenses. In one month she turned her financial reality around dramatically, and she had a plan to pay off her credit card debts. She stopped living in fear about her finances.

In the third month, we focused on how she allocated her time. She kept a time log to identify when she was doing something that aligned with her goals and when she was wasting time. It became clear where her bad habits were with regard to how she used her time. Instead of watching what she called "boring television shows to zone out," she began to use LinkedIn in to identify people she wanted to meet. She invited people in her organization and industry to have tea, to attend an association meeting, or to go for a walk with her. She built new relationships, and she felt her own sense of accomplishment increase dramatically.

Recently, a year and a half after we first began working together, Emily and I met. She is a vibrant, confident, thin, sophisticated woman who is influential beyond her wildest dreams because she had the self-management muscles to focus on creating what was most important to her. She set up a schedule for us to meet twice a year to review where she is and what she wants to focus on next. She is a self-management superstar now!

Your self-management skills are obvious to others, whether you know it or not. Whom do you spend time with? Look closely at your friends and family members. It helps to surround yourself with people who have strong self-management skills. If your friends are health conscious, you are likely to be as well. If your friends are financially free, you will likely become financially free too. Self-management weeds a bad habit out and enables you to positively influence the people in your life.

Teamwork

When people work well together, it is obvious that they care about each other. They understand each other's strengths and blind spots. They want to add value to each other and cover each other's blind spots without highlighting them.

When you serve on a team, do you seek out your peers to get to know them, to understand what motivates them? Do you phrase requests of them in ways that will be interesting and inspiring to them?

Have you ever served on a high-performing team? What was happening on the team?

Dr. Bruce Wayne Tuckman is an American psychologist who has carried out research into the theory of group dynamics. He is currently a professor of educational psychology at the Ohio State University, and he has created a useful model to understand the stages of team development:

Stage 1. Forming
Stage 2. Storming
Stage 3. Norming
Stage 4. Performing
Stage 5. Adjourning

Groups will return to the Forming stage whenever there is a change in the group's goals or team members. Many groups get stuck in one stage; only 29 percent of teams ever reach the Performing stage. Reaching Stage 4 and being a high-performing group requires regular attention to team maintenance as well as task functions.

In my master's degree program, which focused on organization dynamics and group development, I built on this model, and I have been using it with coaching clients to help them navigate both building teams and serving as a team member with their own peers.

Stage 1. Forming

Common feelings of new team members may include these:

- Excitement and optimism about being part of the team
- Pride at being selected to be on the team
- Tentative about attachment to this new group: Will they accept me?
- Anxiety about the tasks ahead and fear of failure: Will the people on the team have the skills to do what needs to be done?

What the team leader needs to do during the Forming stage:

- Help people get to know each other.
- Identify and prioritize the goals and vision for the group.
- Surface hopes, fears, and expectations.
- Establish ground rules for independent action, participation, resolving conflict, presenting ideas, and reaching consensus.

- Identify the roles and responsibilities of the team members and ensure that they understand them.
- Hold meetings focused on having the team members share their preferred communication style and workplace motivators, and how they like to add value to the team.
- Make decisions, and do not expect the team members to be able to make decisions together on their own yet.

Stage 2. Storming

Common feelings of team members during the Storming stage may include these:

- Frustration at lack of progress
- Anxiety over miscommunication and problems with teamwork
- Fear of different communication styles and working with people who are very different from one another
- Fluctuations between optimism and pessimism about the group's chances of succeeding

It is common to see these types of behaviors when a team is in the Storming stage:

- Resistance to the purpose, goals, tasks, and processes
- Arguing among team members
- Staking out areas of expertise
- Forming subgroups
- Complaining about the workload
- Resisting leadership and influence from others

What the team leader needs to do during the Storming stage:

- Surface underlying issues; encourage the expression of feelings and possible solutions to the issues.
- Define the roles and accountabilities of the team members and play to each team member's strengths.

- Create subgroups to make decisions, but mix subgroup members; focus on major issues with the entire group together.
- Model listening skills to every member of the team, not just favorite members.
- Be solution focused; ask questions that focus on what the team leader wants to create.
- Make decisions and move through conflict; don't keep conflicts alive for long periods of time.
- Do not ignore the conflicts; that will cause them to get bigger.

Stage 3. Norming

Common feelings of team members during the Norming stage may include these:

- Relief that the tension and conflict have subsided
- Renewed confidence in the team's abilities
- Increased willingness to be seen as a team member
- Willing to give and receive developmental feedback; more open to listen
- Increased caring for members of the team

It is common to see these types of behaviors when a team is in the Norming stage:

- Enforce group norms and standards.
- Communicate more openly and directly.
- Cooperate with a focus on group goals.
- Negotiate rather than compete for resources.
- Test for and build group consensus.
- Share feelings and personal issues; be more authentic and real with each other.
- Give overt attention to the team's maintenance needs and functions.

What the team leader needs to do during the Norming stage:

- Speak the hidden norms, and help the team to evaluate and set new norms.
- Help the team to develop a unique identity.
- Challenge the team members' boundaries individually.
- Coach the team members in building new skills and sharing what they know.
- Use consensus building and explore areas of difference.
- Invite input and feedback on every major decision.
- Let the team members make some decisions on their own together.

Stage 4. Performing

Common feelings of team members during the Performing stage may include these:

- Acceptance of each other's strengths and developmental areas
- Trust in the others and willingness to be vulnerable
- Comfort in dealing with differences and resolving conflict
- Pride in being part of the team

It is common to see these types of behaviors when a team is in the Performing stage:

- Team members adapt their style to meet the needs of the project at the time.
- Influence is multilateral within the group.
- Team members openly communicate thoughts and feelings.
- Everyone has a voice and is heard.
- Conflict is managed and resolved. Differences are encouraged and discussed.
- Team members enjoy collaborating.
- Coaching feedback is given and received at the deepest levels because trust is so high.

- Members identify strongly with the team, and they have deep pride in the accomplishments of the team.

What the team leader needs to do during the Performing stage:

- Sit back and enjoy! Let them lead!
- Use consensus for all major team decisions.
- Give lots of positive feedback.
- Experiment and explore process improvements.
- Encourage the group to develop evaluation criteria. Do not do the work for the team.
- Celebrate and affirm accomplishments.
- Arrange ceremonies for closure and for assimilating new members into the group.

Stage 5. Adjourning

Common feelings of team members during the Adjourning stage may include these:

- Apprehension over loss of group identity
- Pride in the group's achievements
- Reluctance to let go
- Regret over any poorly managed conflicts or endings

It is common to see these types of behaviors when a team is in the Adjourning stage:

- Evaluating results and producing final status reports
- Being willing or unwilling to let go
- Wanting recognition and appreciation
- Saying good-bye and having conversations for closing

What the team leader needs to do during the Adjourning stage:

- Establish closing procedures for the team.
- Discuss endings with team members individually and as a group.
- Provide a way for team members to acknowledge what they appreciate about each other.
- End with a ritual that honors the group and each of its members.

Written Communication

E-mail, memos, proposals, instructions, text messages, and reports all require writing. Every professional role requires written communication. Writing keeps business moving, and it enables messages to be shared across organizations, communities, and countries quickly.

It takes most business executives at least an hour to create a typical business letter. You will not be able to communicate your ideas or be seen as a high performer if you cannot create compelling written communications. Also, as a manager, you will be communicating at times with your star performers in writing, which will be great opportunities for you to demonstrate what outstanding writing looks like in your organizational culture.

Effective writing requires careful planning to be as clear and persuasive as possible. Whether you are sending a simple e-mail to a coworker in the office next to yours or a proposal to your most important customer, your writing will be more effective if you answer these questions before you begin:

- Whom do I want to read what I am writing?
- What is my purpose for writing this? (Answer in one sentence.)
- What is my core message? What is most important for readers to understand from my writing?
- What is the right style and tone for this communication?
- What format will be most effective?

Writing well is a dynamic process that enables you to discover and reevaluate your own thinking as your work evolves. As you write, you may become clearer in your own thinking just from the act of putting your words into a document. Revising and polishing are vital if clarity is to emerge in written materials. Some people do not want to put in the time to revise and review, which is unfortunate because such efforts could ultimately save them time. I have found that it takes a lot of time to clean up miscommunication that occurs when people do not take the time to write clearly in their first attempt.

Planning an important document includes these steps:

- Pulling together all the key ideas and messages you want to convey. I put each of these onto a separate Post-it note and hang it on the wall next to my computer.
- Brainstorming additional ideas that the readers of the document will want covered.
- Creating an outline that has a flow—that is, a sequence—of ideas that build and connect logically and that will be understood by the audience.
- Allotting as much time to revising and editing as you do to planning a letter, report, or proposal. When you think you are finished, reread your document, and ask yourself the following questions:
  - Is this the right level for my audience?
  - Is my purpose for writing this clear in the beginning?
  - Does my core message come through clearly? Is what is most important highlighted concisely?
  - Did I create the right style and tone for this communication?
  - Is this format effective?

Consider reading *Successful Writing at Work* by Philip Kolin. Adding this book to your resources library will aid you when you have a writing project that is overwhelming.

Sometimes it is better to pick up the phone or go meet in person because some things do not belong in writing. Let me give you an example: Rajan was newly assigned to a project that was already underway. He was helping to file the paperwork after a national sales meeting that had required a physician as a speaker. In this case, because the company was paying a physician to speak at a pharmaceutical meeting, it was vital to have a contract indicating that the doctor was being paid to educate the audience, not to exclusively represent the pharmaceutical company. Rajan's boss sent him an e-mail saying, "Find the contract." Rajan was very concerned because the contract was nowhere to be found. He e-mailed his boss to inform him of this fact. The boss, who was on vacation at the time, wrote back, "Maybe we could just ask the speaker to re-sign a new contract and postdate it to before the event."

Rajan did not know if postdating the contract was legal, so he wrote back to his boss and asked him. Rajan's boss e-mailed, "If we value our jobs, we need a contract now." Rajan interpreted this as a threat and wrote back, "Not only do I value the job I have, but I also value my future roles and want to do the right thing legally."

In the subsequent debriefing on this escalated issue, it was very clear that both Rajan and his boss wanted to do the right thing, and they were not understanding each other in the back-and-forth e-mails. This e-mail exchange should have stopped as soon as one of them felt it was an emotional or complex issue. That is the time to pick up the phone or make an appointment to meet in person to discuss the details. An e-mail can be written after the meeting to summarize and confirm what they agreed to.

Brett M. Saks, vice president of human resources, kgb USA, has shared, "Exemplary communication skill (both written and verbal) is often touted as the critical item that all professionals need in order to grow their careers in an organization. It's also often identified as a predictor for advancement; if you can communicate clearly, concisely, and influentially, you have a shot at the C suite, regardless of other shortcomings."

Index

Star Developer Award

Do you know someone who is already amazing at developing high performers in your organization?

Would you like to acknowledge that person for his or her contribution to you and your organization?

Would you consider nominating that person for the Star Developer Award?

This is an honor that will be given on October 3 each year. This date was selected to honor the birthday of someone who has made a profoundly positive impact on my life, Elizabeth Jeffries, CPAE. To nominate someone for this award, please write a letter of nomination indicating how this person impacted your organization by developing high potential performers.

To learn more about this award and nomination process, please go to www.TheProfessionalDevelopmentGroup.com/StarDeveloperAward.

Would you like to participate in this event? You'll find details on the website.

Shawn Kent Hayashi is a coach, speaker, author, and consultant. She is the founder of The Professional Development Group, serving clients including entrepreneurs, academic organizations, and Fortune 500 companies: Johnson & Johnson, the Federal Reserve Bank, American Express, and Alvarez Orthodontics, to name just a few. You'll quickly discover that her message appeals to all businesses because she herself has been a leader in large and small organizations. She has served on the boards of directors of several organizations including the advisory board for the University of Pennsylvania, where she received her Masters in Organization Dynamics. She has had the honor of speaking at hundreds of conferences and corporate functions and she has been featured in *BusinessWeek, Chief Learning Officer, Forbes, The Globe and Mail, Momentum, The Philadelphia Business Journal, Training,* and on HR.com. Shawn is passionate about developing star performers, and that shows in everything she does.